Merry Christmas
to brother Stuart
with much love
from
Margaret and Ben
1987

Ray Barrette is in his
late eighties — a charming
friend of ours.

A Countryman's Bed-Book

A Countryman's Bed-Book

More Observations on Country Matters from Amen Farm

By Roy Barrette

DOWN EAST BOOKS

ISBN 0-89272-235-5
Library of Congress Catalog Card No. 86-72983
Cover design and illustration by Michael McCurdy
Printed at The Book Press, Brattleboro, Vt.

2 4 5 3 1

Down East Books
Box 679, Camden, Maine 04843

Contents

The Garden and the Land

Getting Away

Matters of the Spirit

I dedicate this book to all who love the world we live in, its bluebirds and bobolinks, its snowstorms and summer skies, its sunrises and moonlit nights. Cherish it and clutch every moment to you, for we are all but tenants soon to be dispossessed.

"Dream of no heaven but that which lies about you."
— Henry Thoreau

Acknowledgments

I owe a debt to several people that I would, here, with gratitude acknowledge. To Russell Wiggins, publisher and editor of the *Ellsworth American*, and to Lawrence K. Miller, publisher of the *Berkshire Eagle* and *UpCountry,* I give thanks for their encouragement to reprint these columns and articles that first appeared under their auspices. To Lorraine Hanson, who typed and helped select and arrange what is here written, I am more than grateful. To Richard B. Davidson and *Down East* Magazine I offer particular thanks for permission to use the Prologue, which rekindles a memory of raindrops dimpling the waters of Lake Megunticook so many years ago. And, as always, to my wife—who, when I told her we were coming to Maine to live, said only, "When do we start?"—my love.

Foreword

This book is, in a sense, a sequel to a previous book, *A Countryman's Journal,* which is a collection of essays about my farm and the village in which I live. But it is not wholly so. When I wrote the first book, I was younger and Amen Farm was a working unit with cattle and sheep, and pigs and turkeys, all calling for daily attention. Today, the larger animals are gone and the only inhabitants of the barn are a few dozen hens. The number of those who live in the farmhouse has also been diminished by the death of my wife's mother at age ninety-four, but we live on, with our two dogs, and watch the peaceful years pass by.

When I came to Maine and bought a tumbledown house over-looking the lower reaches of Blue Hill Bay, I satisfied the desire of a lifetime. I had been born in the country, but, after an adventurous youth, had spent most of my middle life employed in the world's great cities. I had not chosen my career; it had grown on me by a succession of unplanned events. Most would say that fortune smiled upon me, and I would not dispute them, but I had always kept in mind a dream of returning, someday, to my beginnings, to rural surroundings. I succeeded beyond my expectations, for my house, in addition to being in quiet country, is within sight, sound, and smell of the sea where I was nurtured as a young man. I am the happiest of men, and the most grateful, because after the passage of a quarter of a century I am still here where there has been little change since that first morning I watched the rising sun etch sharp the spruces on the offshore islands. I still can feel the soft sea wind as it stirs the leaves of the beeches and watch the hummingbirds pause in mid-flight over the scarlet geraniums in my window boxes while, high above, a seagull rides the crest of the rising wind.

I say this book is not wholly a sequel because it is more a matter of "reperusals and recollections" than a recounting of current daily events, as was the first one. It is a collection of remembrances, of thoughts, *pensées,* of small happinesses that have come to me over a long life. I share them with you in the hope that some of the pleasure I have had may be yours also.

Some men draw their life from urban surroundings, the press of humanity and the ceaseless hum of the city. They agree with Sidney Smith, who said, "I have no relish for the country; it is a kind of healthy grave." But there are others of us who believe with William Cowper that "God made the country, man made the town." Many of the latter are not so fortunate as I and are compelled to live in city or suburb all their lives. It is for these, people who are countrymen at heart, no matter where they live, that I have written a weekly newspaper column for the past twenty years, trying, in simple words, to bring the country to them, particularly my own small part of it.

The appeal of rural life is more than sheep and cows and woods and fields, or town meetings and village affairs; it is the philosophy the country engenders. It is a view of life that grows out of small things, personal day-to-day happenings that are not overwhelmed by impersonal events about which most have us have no real knowledge and little control. I once wrote that man's biggest barrier, a mental one, in his search for happiness was his trampling on the manna laid at his feet every day while in search of greater miracles. I try to convey in my writing a sense of tranquility. I write of simple things and small occurrences because when the captains and the kings have departed, and our gods are but an ancient memory, the humble mind will be as it has always been. The country will be unchanged. Gulls will cry down the wind; the foxes will have their dens, and mothers will still shelter their children while fathers stand between them and harm.

I want my readers to hear me and be by my side, sharing my thoughts and surroundings. Time has robbed me of vigor, but there are compensations: more time for the closer observation and consideration of small matters—things that constitute the bulk of our experiences whether we be famous or unknown. I take a quiet pleasure in watching the colored reflections of a crystal prism hanging in my library window as, slowly circling, they move across the walls and ceiling ("Rainbows!" my delighted great-granddaughter said as she tried in vain to grasp them). I love the fog that steals in from the ever-restless sea, an enveloping visitor that comes as silently as time passes. I love the early morning sunlight reflected from the waters of the bay onto the ceiling of my small bedroom. After all these years I am still moved by the beauty of the long shadows cast by the setting sun and I am struck by the appearance it gives the white lighthouse, as though its buildings were cut from cardboard and pasted onto the backdrop of sea and mountains. Truly, I feel I can say with the psalmist: "The lines are fallen unto me in pleasant places; yea, I have a goodly heritage."

I was coming home yesterday over a route I have traveled a thousand times, my conscious attention bent on driving, when suddenly the road was transformed from its customary familiarity; it assumed a complete freshness, as if I were seeing it for the first time. The experience was exciting and delightful. It was as though I had suddenly been blessed with inner sight, as though I was living on two levels of understanding. I was uplifted by my clarity of vision. The clumps of alders, the roadside birches, the darkness of the spruces, even the shadows cast by the banks of snow where they had been thrust aside by the plows, were interesting and strangely novel. Henry Thoreau once said that he had traveled far, in Concord. What he meant was that a man did not have to *go* anywhere to see the world, that it was always there before him. All he needed was to be sighted. I think that the paths Thoreau traveled around Concord were always new, though familiar, to him and that he saw them as I saw the road into the village yesterday. It is these small moments of insight that I try to capture in the hope that the recounting of them may give pleasure to the reader. Addison said, "True happiness is of a retired nature and an enemy to pomp and noise." I avoid pomp and noise.

This book is called *A Countryman's Bed-Book* because it should be taken in homeopathic doses. The prescription reads, "Two or three essays to be taken each night before retiring." I hope you read in bed. Most of the pieces have appeared before in newspapers, although many have been rewritten, changed, abridged, or added to in order to suit the somewhat different demands of a book. However, the purpose of writing remains the same: it is an effort on the author's part to allow the readers to look through his eyes and understand how he feels about something they may not have had the time or opportunity to see and think about for themselves.

Prologue

When we were very small, the Mack brothers and I, who adventured together in all sorts of ways, took up fishing.We made our first fishing rods in the time-honored way, out of bamboo poles with string tied to the ends, and rode our bikes to the pond on Frogtown Road a mile from our homes in Connecticut, and had no luck.

We concluded, in a modern American way, that our equipment was at fault, saved up our allowances, and bought "real" fishing rods at Breslow Brothers' store. I think my first fishing rod and reel together cost four dollars—a solid sum for those days.

With "real" equipment and lots of worms, our luck turned slightly better. I caught a perch. It was eight inches long and looked lonely on the serving dish after my mother cooked it. Each member of the family got one square inch as his portion.

I caught very few fish, and they were tiny. They did not leap up out of the water like the rainbow trout on the covers of *Outdoor Life,* did not shake shining beads of sunlit water out in a raging arc behind them, did not fight like the dickens. In fact, they never broke the surface, and they came to the water's edge with disappointing docility, almost as if they were tiny pet dogs and all I had to do was whistle for them to come home.

But the dream of the great fish striking, leaping, fighting, stayed with me, and in the summer of 1950 my father took the family on our first vacation in Maine. I was nine. I knew that in Maine there were real fish—trout and bass, pickerel and pike—the kind that made those leaps onto the covers of *Outdoor Life* and *Field and Stream.*

While we were in Maine, a business friend and colleague of my father's called and invited us to visit him on his island in Lake Megunticook. There was, he said, a peninsula near him that was for sale; perhaps my father and mother would like to look at it. We went. It was a gray day, a perfect fishing day, and nothing up to that time (and very few things since) excited me more than Lake Megunticook on a perfect fishing day.

Dark forests of hemlock and spruce on the shores; mist-covered mountains all around. Deep, dark, quiet waters. Quiet, dour, middle-aged men trolling by the cliff's edge with heavy line and copper leaders, going after the landlocked salmon. Salmon!

My father broke the agony of suspense and said yes, he wanted to buy that property, and the great gift of my tenth birthday was to know that we had a place on this lake, that all my life stretched before me as a time when I too could go after the trout, bass, pickerel, and salmon in a lake more beautiful than anything I had seen in my magazines.

That winter my father bought me a fly rod. My school days were a matter of marking time until I could use it to go after those fish in Megunticook. But when summer finally did come, I began my first cruel lessons in real fishing. I snapped flies off the end of the line, hung them in alder bushes. In desperation, I went back to worms and caught perch no bigger nor more ferocious that the docile ones in the pond on Frogtown Road.

My father's colleague, from his island nearby, must have sensed my frustration. Perhaps I told him. In any case, he could see very easily the panorama of my ignorance and frustration, and one day offered to take me fishing. He knew this lake "pretty well," he said; he could show me a few tricks and take me to some places where I would have better luck.

He rowed over and picked me up at seven the next morning. A small man, but strong, he rowed with the ease that comes from long years of experience. It was raining, and the mist was closed down over the mountaintops, the black surface of the lake pocked with raindrops. He had on a khaki rain suit and a drooping rain hat with two or three flies hooked into the band. I vaguely noticed that although he had said "we" would go fishing together, he had not brought his own fishing rod.

He spoke kindly but with immense authority: "The first thing is that we have to be quiet." That was rugged duty for the ten-year-old I was then; excitement seemed to pump loud exclamations out of me when all I'd intended to do was whisper.

A COUNTRYMAN'S BED-BOOK

Off he rowed. We'll wait until we get to the right spot, he said. *Wait?* I couldn't wait. Quietly and with authority he explained to me that learning to fish meant learning to wait. While we rowed, he talked to me about a perfect day of fishing he once had, during which he hadn't even gotten a bite. What? At first, I didn't understand at all.

He rowed patiently, rhythmically. Yes, fishing is much more, he explained, than the trophy fish. It is being quiet, learning to wait, learning to be part of the water and the landscape, in nature rather than invading it.

Finally, he reached over, took the end of the long leader on my fly rod, brought out a knife and nipped the end neatly, picked one of the wet flies from the band in his hat, and showed me how to tie it on properly. You must, he said, do it properly. Then he snipped it off and had me do it. I do not remember how many times it took to do it properly, but I do know that the fly did not go into the water until it was affixed right.

It was a wet fly, he explained, and we would troll with it, because this was the kind of day when that was proper to do. And now we would be quiet.

On and on he went, quietly—over to the rocky shore off Lutz's Island. Softly, softly he rowed. I sat there, perhaps beginning to understand a little.

And right now, today, thirty years later, I can row you over from our peninsula to the exact spot where the smallmouth bass struck that fly in a rush, shot in toward the shore, fought for its life while a dry-throated little boy began to bring it in.

What I remember most is the voice of the man who was teaching me. Quiet. It infused me. Quiet instructions every exiting stage of the way. Give a little now. Take a little now. Be calm. Here he is. We'll net him soon. Be calm.

It was not, I think, the biggest fish I was ever to catch. If memory serves, and if I can resist the fisherman's impulse to exaggerate, it was about eighteen inches long and a little over two pounds. But it surely was the best, because it was the first real fish caught properly, the first to be part of the proper ritual, the first to fight so well that if I had not brought it in *well,* I could not have brought it in at all.

There are in our lives, I think, a few special scenes that take on the qualities of a tableau. We paint them in our memories, stand outside, and paint ourselves into them. I have painted in my memory a canvas characterized by gentle colors—gray of mist, black of water, khaki of clothes, green-brown of the fish. My painting has no title, but it partakes of those great scenes wherein the protégé begins to sense the mentor's wisdom, the initiate begins to feel the shaman's power of magic, the little boy begins to understand what the teacher is generous enough to share.

Over the years, the little boy in the painting and the man who rowed him about the lake and taught him something of patience and quietness and propriety went on and apart. The boy went off to boarding school and college and teaching jobs out west; the man—his name is Roy Barrette—sold his island on Megunticook, "retir'd" to Amen Farm in Brooklin, Maine, and became a farmer, gardener, swapper of eggs for bread—and, most of all, a writer.

And you may imagine what it was like to be a professor of English, living and teaching out in Idaho, and to receive a clipping from back home in Maine: an essay by a writer known as "The Retir'd Gardener," whose weekly column appears in the *Ellsworth American* and who has just published a book. In that essay was a voice that spoke quietly, with authority. It spoke of nature, of being *in* it rather than invading it; it spoke of what is proper; it spoke of patience.

I recognized it instantly, for I had heard it, many years before, in the rain, on a lake in Maine.

—Richard B. Davidson

A COUNTRYMAN'S BED-BOOK

Seasons

Sing a song of seasons;
Something bright in all;
Flowers in the summer;
Fires in the fall.

— R. L. Stevenson, 1885

A Devil in the Closet

The clock was just striking five and the sun was already high above Western Mountain when Gay, my Brittany, jumped on the bed, telling me it was time to get up. The bay was a shimmering field of silver, and, early as it was, the swallows were scooping up black flies and mosquitoes and a robin was hard at work extracting an unwilling worm from the dewy lawn. Whenever she flew to her nest on top of the pergola, I could see a clutch of gaping yellow mouths open like so many jacks-in-the-box. Far down the bay I could distinguish a couple of lobster boats in the sheen where they were hauling traps. You have to be up early to be ahead of a lobsterman. Closer at hand, one of our new lambs standing on a boulder between me and the sun was haloed about like the figure of Christ on resurrection morning. I asked myself, as I have many times before, what I had done to deserve such felicity. I found no answer.

I must confess to being a contented man, one who would like to be remembered as a man who was well satisfied with his friends and with the country in which fate set him down. If you believe in the teachings of Christianity you count yourself free to make choices, but if you dislike being responsible for your actions, you hide behind the theories of modern sociologists who hold that free will is nonsense. No credit is allowed for the good things you do, but excuses are offered if you bludgeon and rob some old lady, on the grounds that you were deprived as a child or have been watching too-violent crime dramas on TV. I grew up in a time when it was allowed that there were alternatives. Regardless of your background, it was assumed you knew right from wrong, and which you chose was your own responsibility. Of course, in those days there was a devil lurking in the closet on whom you could blame temptation, but that did not excuse you if you succumbed to his wiles.

Over the years I have done what I could, in an admittedly solitary and unorganized way, to spread such cheer as my opportunities and abilities permitted. I have not devoted myself to a "cause," which seems to be the criterion by which good works are judged—I'm pretty well convinced that the pursuit of great causes usually brings about other evils as large as those it is intended to alleviate. It is so easy to become singleminded by mass action that one becomes afflicted with tunnel vision.

It is not the collapse of empires or the victories of politicians that bring tears to the eyes or laughter to the lips. It is the small, humble, everyday happenings that we live with constantly: the Grange suppers, or picking up a kid thumbing a ride home from school. If you live in the country you know them all by sight, or at least by family resemblance. You rejoice with, or maybe envy, the man who gets the first peas or corn from his garden, and wonder about a granite boulder with the single word "Beulah" inscribed on it in the old graveyard. You enjoy equally the hazy sunset of a smoky sou'wester or the cold steel of a winter sunrise. It is the small things that are important. The bread of life is baked from the fine flour of everyday living, and we live on a poor diet if we forget it.

The pursuit of happiness is something guaranteed us by our laws—or perhaps I should say the right to pursue happiness, which is something else. It is an individual right, and it cannot be served up to the citizenry on demand by law or fiat. A man has to be capable of pursuit before he can effect capture. Too many people do not know what they are attempting to pursue, and would not recognize it if they found it.

The pursuit of happiness is not the same thing as a search for contentment, and contentment is to happiness as the ocean to a puddle. A child may be happy with a new toy or a man with a new mistress, but the emotion is as impermanent as summer lightning. The child breaks the one and the man tires of the other. We hear much about the right to do one's own thing, to seek happiness in one's own way, but the singleminded pursuit of happiness is apt to develop into hedonism, which is the doctrine that pleasure or happiness is the highest good. A man may be happy but not contented, whereas a contented man is happy with a great undercurrent of strength that carries away the daily disappointments that ruffle the surface of every man's existence.

I have always admired the substance of the Quaker philosophy expressed by George Fox, who said, "Be still and cool in thy own mind and spirit," and George Santayana's "It is not wisdom to be only wise and on the inward vision close the eyes."

It isn't only on fine spring mornings that a feeling of contentment assails me. Every time I step into the garden, away from the hurried world, I agree with Louise Driscoll that "Wise men, wise man / Things that grow / Have some power / That you do not know." It revitalizes the soul, and because the nurturing of a plant is my pursuit of happiness, contentment engulfs me in the warmth of the spirit. I don't regard my life as simply the turn of a wheel. Part of it I know is luck, but most of it is because of a decision I made a long time ago to give up some things in order to obtain others. As Samuel Johnson said: "Sir, we know our will is free, and there's an end on't." The will to contentment is every man's choice.

A Solitary Sunrise

In March the days grow appreciably longer. When I get up about 6:30 in the morning, the sun is above the horizon—though sometimes behind a bank of clouds, so that its rays shine upward like those in religious pictures of Easter morning—and we drink our afternoon tea by daylight.

I am not an enthusiastic sunrise servicer. The last one I attended was held some years ago, at our little harbor on Naskeag Point. It was not very inspiring. There were twenty of thirty of us, bundled up against a raw easterly wind that fingered through the heaviest clothing. The sky was gray and overcast, and the only way we knew when the sun rose was because the Nautical Almanac had provided us with the information. There were a couple of fishermen messing about with their boats, but no other nonparticipants. The clammers were not there because the tide was not right, and the scallopers had gone out earlier. Naskeag Harbor is a working refuge, and even in the summer, few except fishermen or locals are to be seen.

The preacher from our village church was there with his zither, and he and his wife led the singing. We sang "When Morning Gilds the Skies" and several other old hymns that reminded me of my childhood, when everyone's schoolday began with a hymn and a prayer. In one of my schools there was a little Jewish boy who sang "Onward Christian Soldiers" as lustily as the rest of us. We envied him; he took all the Christian holidays and the Jewish ones too. We used to ask him about what they did in the Jewish "church" on Saturdays. I was particularly interested in the Ark. I had seen his church and I couldn't figure out how they got the ark and all the animals into that small building. I guess

I thought it must be some sort of Hebrew miracle. I had been brought up on miracles, and it didn't seem any more preposterous than some of the Christian ones.

I think the idea of sunrise services is all to the good, even if I don't go to many of them. It is the only time some people are ever up early enough to see the sun rise. They don't know what they are missing. About the only time I don't witness the dawn is in midsummer, when in this latitude the sky begins to brighten a little after three a.m.

There is something about the world when the sun peeps over the horizon that is as delicate as the velvet on a rose petal. It doesn't last long—half an hour, perhaps—and then you must wait until the next morning to experience it again. The magic is, though, that it happens every day even when no sunrise is visible. Everything is reborn and every little vagrant puff of air makes a wonder of every trembling dew drop on the tip of every tiny blade of grass.

Daniel Webster, who had something to say about everything, had this to say about the sunrise: "The morning itself, few inhabitants of cities know anything about. Among all our good people, not one in a thousand sees the sun rise once a year. They know nothing of the morning. Their idea of it is that it is that part of the day which comes along after a cup of coffee and a piece of toast. . . . The first streak of light, the earliest purpling of the east, which the lark springs up to greet, and the deeper and deeper coloring into orange and red 'til at length the glorious sun is seen, regent of the day—this they never enjoy for they never see it. . . . We see as fine risings of the sun as ever Adam saw: and its risings are as much a miracle now as they were in his day. . . ."

I have the good fortune to live in a house that faces due east, so all I have to do to witness the rising of the sun is to look across ten miles of water to the hills and mountains of the offshore islands. I do it every blessed day of my life. It is the time to get out and breathe deeply of the dawn. I love to watch the little clouds that float above the horizon gradually take on the character of goldfish swimming lazily in the light of a sun that will soon make them invisible in its blinding splendor.

At the winter solstice, when the sun is farthest south, it comes up behind Pond Island, pretty much southeast. On March 21 it will rise over the hills behind Bass Harbor, directly in front of me. When it is welcoming the first of the tourists in June it will have reached its northern limit and will be gilding the spruces on Western Mountain. Each morning I shall celebrate my solitary sunrise service.

A Swallow Away

March 21 is the day of the vernal equinox, the day when the sun crosses the equator on its way north. This is, of course, all in your head, because the sun stays where it has been for quite a while and the crossing is caused by the earth's movement, not the sun's. According to the almanac, spring arrives in the northern hemisphere on March 21. This may be true enough celestially, but not here on earth—at least not at Naskeag Point, Maine. I have irrefutable evidence to the contrary. On the twenty-first of March we often have snow on the ground, or if it happens to be bare, the frost is four feet deep and a northeast gale tears the shingles from the roof and blows through the banking into the cellar, lifting the rugs in the living room. The blast comes, as one of my friends avers, "Right off them damn icebergs."

While age has its disadvantages, it is not entirely without compensations. I can remember when a delayed spring caused me to worry and fret about my garden. I am no longer afflicted in this manner. I know from experience that a few warm and sunny days early in March don't mean an early summer, and I realize that if April comes in on a snowstorm it doesn't mean the year is going to consist of the Fourth of July and winter. The seasons are quite likely to vary markedly from year to year, so that in order to find an accurate mean date, one has to arrive at that average over an extended period. The time is only incidentally related to the vernal equinox. Our first sign of spring at Amen Farm is when the lambs begin to drop at the end of April. It may be that lambs are properly born in February so they will be heavier by autumn, but I don't like acting as midwife to complaining ewes in February so I have a compact with Ralph (our resident tup) that determines the time of the lambs' appearance pretty accurately, and it is not in February.

Of course the real date of spring's arrival, romantic, poetic, and all that, is when the first swallows volplane through the gable window in the north end of the barn. Ours don't show up on the minute like those that shower their blessings on the Mission of San Juan Capistrano—on average the first scouts get here about May 1. They inspect the place to make sure the barn window has been removed and there is enough water in the pond for them to make mud pies to plaster nests with, and we hurry around deploying sheets of plastic over the equipment stored under their nests. You can't housebreak a swallow.

I asked old Roy Bowden if the swallows had been around as long as he had and he allowed that they had. I'd guess they have shared quarters with whoever has lived here ever since the place was built in 1852. I think there were more of them when we kept cattle, but just sheep and hens and turkeys seem to attract enough insects to keep the swallows happy. Even if the population is a bit thin in the spring, the air is thick with birds come fall after a couple of broods have been added.

Ivar brought a barn swallow in to me this morning. It had a broken wing, and rested in his hand without making any effort to get away. I hope Butterscotch, our yellow cat, didn't get it, and I doubt he did, even though he is indeed a mighty hunter before the Lord. About the only time he catches a swallow is in hot weather when they spread their wings on the ground to do a little dusting. Most of the time they are too fast, and dive bomb and torment him unmercifully.

We don't usually think of birds having accidents, but they do. I don't mean being struck by a car, but mischances that come about because their navigational computers malfunction. Swallows swoop low over ponds and pastures to collect insects and occasionally hit the surface. They frequently touch the water in a pond with their wingtips, but sometimes they miscalculate or hit a downdraft and take an involuntary ducking. I have seen them swing low out of the barn and hit the gravel in the driveway. I guess their mortality rate is high, but they raise a couple of broods a summer, and because they feed on insects that are not a source of poison like the food of eagles and fish hawks, who live on the end of the food chain, they are not exposed to that danger.

For me there is something particularly rural and peaceful about swallows. The ones I see most often are barn swallows, though there are others: tree swallows nest year after year in the same hole in an old apple tree on our back terrace, and bank swallows live in Grindle's gravel pit. However, barn swallows are the most domesticated. I never see them far from the habitation of man, and I think, like robins, they value our company.

Maybe my association of swallows with rural pursuits originates in my affection for Gilbert White and the Hampshire village of Selborne where he lived and wrote about them. I spent my schooldays near there and perhaps watched the descendants of the birds he saw. I was, like all boys, a bad boy. I collected birds' eggs, and one of my greatest desires was to add a bank swallow's egg to my collection. There were several gravel pits nearby, but the birds are too wise to excavate holes in working pits. What I had to find was one that had been exhausted. But even when I did there were problems. The nest holes were invariably just far enough below the edge that they could not be reached from above, and as the pits were usually partly filled with water, scaling the steep bank from the bottom was hazardous. I never did get an egg, and when, the other day, I saw some holes just over the edge of one of Grindle's old workings, I was moved to consider making one more try. I never did, though. Age is a great impediment to adventure. Apart from the probability that I would have fallen over the edge into the pit, I wondered what my friends driving by would have thought of an octogenarian columnist hanging head-down in a gravel pit collecting birds' eggs.

A Wisp of Fog

The first thing I do every morning when I wake up is swing open my skylight window (which is hinged in the middle) and look down the bay. (At least, I do so after I sit on the edge of the bed a few minutes to adjust my equilibrium so I won't fall on my face when I stand on my feet.) When I opened it this morning, fog rolled in like steam from a boiling cauldron and I could not see across the road, let alone the ten miles to Bass Harbor Light. It was still a little before six o'clock so the sun was not yet above the horizon, but even so there was a predawn luminescence to the fog. I guessed it would burn off by ten o'clock, and it did, but the day did not turn clear—the sky remained hazy and the horizon existed only in the imagination rather than in reality.

Only a few sails dotted the water east of Green Island. Summer folk who spend their time on the water grow knowledgeable about the weather, wiser more often than the forecasters. On days that threaten fog they stay ashore. On a foggy Sunday our church has a full congregation, but the call of the Lord is more muted when there is bright sun and wind out of the northwest.

Fog is a fact of life for those who live on the coast. It can steal in off the ocean at any time but does so more frequently in the summer, particularly during July and August. Morning fog often retreats before noon, but you can see it hanging offshore like a second horizon, waiting to tiptoe back in when the sun sets and the land cools. Here on Naskeag Point, with water all around us, we are often fogged in when three miles up the road in the village the sun is shining. Fog does not always lift with the sun and can set in solidly for three or four days on end, which makes visitors to Maine who have only a week's vacation wonder. I recall entertaining guests from Mexico City, where there is never fog (pollution maybe, but not fog) and where it rains only on schedule, in the afternoon and then only during the rainy season. It was a lovely evening when they arrived, but by the next morning it was thick-a-fog, a real pea-souper, and stayed that way for the three days of their visit. On the evening before they left we overheard the woman say to her husband, "What a dreadful place. What a dreary and depressing place. How can anyone choose to live here?" Well, if it was foggy all the time there would be some merit to her opinion, but after fog can come those brittle-clear days and nights when the wind is like wine and the stars crackle in the heavens—times we like to think of as typical of Maine.

Fog is usually a blessing, not a curse. It is what keeps our flowers colorful. Never anywhere are they as clear and bright as they are with us. Though we have sunny days, they are never so long continued that the flowers fade. When the thermometer has hovered between eighty and ninety degrees (and it does do that sometimes even here), nothing pleases me more than to see, suddenly, that the shoreline is obscured and to feel the burning heat of the sun quickly fade so the ladies reach for a sweater or shawl, a standard piece of apparel on the coast.

When fog first stretches tentative fingers over the land it is scarcely noticeable. It appears as though cobwebs were floating across the field—as Gilbert White wrote on June 8, 1775, "going abroad early in the morning I found the stubble in the fields matted with filmy webs and witnessed a shower of cobwebs . . . continuing 'till the close of day"—then they lengthen into long diaphanous streamers riding the wind. Eventually the main body envelops us, and the bleating of the sheep is muffled and the rooster's bragging becomes subdued.

Unless fog is heavy and long maintained, our lobstermen go about their lawful occasions as usual. I have watched from the shore as they get into a rowboat that has been riding a haul-off and pull away until they pass from sight. Presently there is the cough of a motor, and they are away to find and haul a string of traps, hoping their trip is worthwhile.

There have been times in my life, running into an unfamiliar anchorage, when I could have done without the added handicap of fog, but now that I am where I can still see and smell salt water but don't have to navigate on it, I count fog's virtues and not its dangers.

Fog is something you learn to live with in coastal Maine. It is one of the verities of life. Perhaps my memory is playing tricks on me, but as I recall there was less discontent over bad weather when I was a boy than there is now. Perhaps it was that people accepted what they had to make the best of, or perhaps the whole attitude toward vacationing was more relaxed. One made one's reservations months ahead and began to pack bags weeks ahead, and when the day to depart finally arrived, the whole family went along, including the dog. Sure it was wonderful if the days were fair beyond belief, as they often were, but the old-fashioned summer hotels were roomy and prepared to cope with weather if it should house-bind the guests. They all had large public rooms where the kids could play ping-pong or badminton. There were long porches, some open and some glassed-in, where older rusticators could creak the hours away in a rocking chair with a book or chat with other guests who had been meeting there for countless summers. A holiday then was not so much going away to see something one had not seen before as it was a quiet break in the year's activities when people had a chance to unwind.

The young never used to mind the fog much, or even the rain unless it was torrential. They put on oilskins and rubber boots, which had been packed and sent ahead in enormous trunks, and wandered along the beach or ledges capturing small crabs hiding under the rockweed or collecting bits of driftwood, "sea glass," horseshoe crab shells, sand dollars, and odd bits of flotsam and jetsam that the ocean is constantly spewing onto the shore. When their stomachs told them it was time for food, they slipped and stumbled up trails through the woods on the way back to the hotel, gathering as they went twigs pendant with lichen and clumps of moss, and if they were lucky, a specimen of the beautiful but deadly amanita with its spotted red cap, or maybe fragile Indian pipes.

It wasn't just fog that gave one time to relax. A vacation meant two or three weeks at a summer hotel or boarding house and an opportunity to become acquainted with the countryside and its inhabitants. True, you had to walk down the hall to the bathroom, and the linoleum was cold on the feet. The drinking water in your room was in a little decanter with a tumbler upended over it to keep out the dust. The beds were iron painted white, the mattresses thin, and the plumbing erratic, but the food was excellent and ample and eaten at a long table with other guests. No one attempted to visit Boothbay Harbor, the windjammer fleet at Camden, Mount Cadillac, and perhaps Rangeley and Jackman all during one vacation. It was assumed that one liked to walk and would get places under foot power. Picnics were well attended, and the solitary car, if there was one, was used to transport food, wood, and the ice cream freezer. The picnickers walked unless disabled or very old, and not many in those days would admit to being so old that they could no longer walk.

There was really not very much to do that would appeal to our sophisticated tourist of today, who counts the day lost that has not added four hundred miles to the speedometer and another travel attraction to his diary. People were more interested in returning to something remembered and loved than in seeing something new. Certainly you can now *ride* to the top of Mount Cadillac and perhaps watch the surf spew into Thunder Hole and admire the view along Ocean Drive. You can eat lobsters plucked from one of the steaming cauldrons alongside the highway and probably purchase one of those tightly packed little sacks of balsam needles to take home and wonder what to do with, all within a couple of days. But the pictures that the mind retains become superimposed upon each other, frequently completely lost if it rained upon your day, and seldom more lasting than the fading scent in the balsam sack.

In the old days, when the holidays were over you knew a lot about a small group of people and had an intimate knowledge of a small section of the country, which I think is better than seeing a lot and not knowing anything. Life was more of a piece and the vagaries of weather taken in stride. Fog was nature's invitation to stop and bide a wee, a time to see inward what was or might be.

Where Wealth Accumulates

Years ago I was given as a birthday present a copy of Oliver Goldsmith's poem, "The Deserted Village." I still own it, a thin yellowed pamphlet bound in hard covers, the eighth edition, which was published in 1775. In his dediction to Sir Joshua Reynolds the author says, "I have taken all possible pains, in my country excursions, for these four or five years past, to be certain of what I alledge: and that all my views and inquiries have led me to believe these miseries real, which I attempt here to display."

I suppose that everyone who has struggled through high school, even in these days when English literature is spurned as having no economic value, is familiar with some parts of "The Deserted Village." They recognize lines like, "Sweet Auburn, loveliest village of the plain, / Where health and plenty cheered the laboring swain," or, "Ill fares the land, to hastening ills a prey, / Where wealth accumulates and men decay."

When Goldsmith wrote he was inveighing against the Enclosure Acts, which allowed the wealthy to fence in and appropriate land that had been the common property of the villagers since time immemorial—land where they had always pastured their animals and cut their hay and bracken. Like William Cobbett, who came later, he was concerned about the concentration of wealth in the cities and the evils attendant upon the flow of people to urban areas, where they were tied to a pay envelope instead of supported by their own independent efforts. He could see the rural population coming under the control of city politicians and the small farmers giving way to large landowners. He anticipated the destruction of the villages, where country people gathered to run their own affairs without the interference of bureaucrats unfamiliar with their problems and antithetical to their philosophies.

Sadly, what Goldsmith feared came to pass; agriculture, in America as in England, is now big business. Small farmers and those in parafarming pursuits have been forced off the land and out of the villages. You do not need statistics to prove this; all you have to do is think how things were, not a hundred years ago but ten or twenty—or if you want a sharper contrast, fifty years ago—times well within your own memory if you are old enough to have served in the Second World War.

In my own village the population 130 years ago was 1002. Thirty years ago it had declined to 656. Today it is about the same but is reinforced during the summer by an equal number of nonresidents. Only seven people were born here last year, and fourteen died, so the downward trend among the resident population continues. Of course, not all of the present residents of the village were born here. I do not have figures on migration, but it is obvious that the native population is gradually being replaced by people like myself who came from other parts. However, even including the newcomers, the total population has barely held its own.

Taxes have *not* remained stationary. In 1850 the total town tax was $1168.26. In 1940 it was $37,193.08. In 1963 (hold on to your hat) it was $239,484.62! The total taxpaying population is, for all practical purposes, unchanged because nonresidents about equal residents in numbers and pay about half the taxes. When I bought my place in 1957 the total town taxes were $46,977.73, and I can see little benefit we have reaped for this sixfold increase. The truth is that much of it has been mandated by the state government and its bureaucracies, which are controlled by the cities—a condition not unique to Maine.

One of the sadder aspects of this domination by city politicians and bureaucrats having no sympathy with nor understanding of rural life is its effect on the older native residents. Inflated taxes are driving out of their homes people whose ancestors tamed the wilderness and built the houses that are the pride of the New England countryside. The bureaucrats say that Ira Perkins must pay the increased taxes they insist be assessed because his property is worth more. Worth more to whom? I would ask. Not to Ira. He still gets exactly the same value out of it that he did fifty years ago or that his ancestors did a hundred and fifty years past: shelter, a garden perhaps, and a few cords of wood. If he protests, the bureaucrats tell him, "If you can't pay the taxes, sell the place and move somewhere else. You can make a good profit." They don't give a damn that his people were born and grew up there for generations. One house or another is all the same to an apartment dweller or suburbanite. In fact, most of them count on moving into a new house every few years. It does something for their ego. It proves that they are "upwardly mobile," in sociologist gobbledegook.

I doubt there is much that can be done about it. They have us licked by weight of numbers. Eighty percent of the population live in the cities and but twenty in the country, but turn over in your mind our scandal-ridden governments, our conglomerates that go around the world bribing all and sundry to obtain business, and the fact that if the lights go out in the cities for a couple of hours, people take to the streets to rob and rape and burn—and consider that maybe Goldsmith had something when he said:

Ill fares the land, to hastening ills a prey,
Where wealth accumulates and men decay.

Autumnal Tints

Although nature is apt to contradict almost any generalization one is unwise enough to give utterance to, I think it is within the bounds of reason to claim that the brilliance and earliness of this autumn's foliage is due to the dry summer. As early as mid-August the trees growing on thin soil underlain by ledge were turning yellow. It was not a happy gold such as the sugar maples bless us with, but a faded and dispirited color with leaves brittle and curling. The first place I noticed it was at the sharp turn in the road in North Brooklin where the dooryard of one house is little else but a granite outcrop (a good place to pile cordwood, as people do around here).

It seems to me that more and more visitors come each year to admire the foliage; and they should, for there are not many places in the world where the phenomenon occurs. Apart from eastern North America, and particularly New England, there are, I believe, only two areas where the same spectacular coloration can be found. One is in China and the other in South America. Our friends from abroad who visit us at this time of year cannot find words to express their delight and amazement. We who live here admire it, but having witnessed the miracle many times before are less apt to go into panegyrics. Even so, I have yet to meet a person, native or visitor, who was not a "leaf peeper," as the hoteliers and moteliers dub those who fill their beds and dining rooms for a couple of weeks in October. In fact, the leaves bring so many travelers that when I once tried, unsuccessfully, to obtain an October reservation at a country inn I learned that some people book as far as a year ahead.

One might think that the species of tree was an important factor in coloration, and to some extent it is, because sugar maples always turn gold, swamp maples red and yellow, and white ash tints of purple, but if those same trees are growing in a different part of the world, even though they retain the same distinctive color, it is a pale ghost of the brilliance we see here in New England.

Once when I was in England in the autumn, I was told that if I would visit Sheffield Park, in Sussex, I would find a beautiful display of autumn foliage. I did, and it was a magnificent garden, an arboretum really, covering a hundred acres. I think it must have contained a specimen of almost every tree hardy in that climate. The most lovely spot was where a lake in the foreground reflected the surrounding trees. They were indeed colored, and the scene was ravishing, but it was though one were looking through a silk screen. All the brilliance was missing, and without the startling contrasts we see here the picture was muted and *triste*. It reminded me of a little book I was given many years ago that is titled *Corners of Grey Old Gardens*. Sheffield Park's great trees, with their sad coloring (sad in the sense our ancestors used to word to signify sober colored), give an impression of immense age and a "grey old garden." (The garden *is* old, too. It was the property of Simon de Montfort in the thirteenth century. While it has nothing to do with autumn coloring, there is a little story told about Simon de Montfort that before the battle of Lewis he exhorted his men to "make a true confession of their sins." He was backed up by the Bishop of Worcester, who told the men that if they fought stoutly the next day, all who died in battle would "gain entrance into the kingdom of Heaven." A hard way to attain paradise.)

If you have it handy or can borrow it from the library, I would recommend to you for pleasant autumn reading Henry Thoreau's long essay, "Autumnal Tints." I have it in a small book called *Excursions,* which was published in 1863, the year after his death. There are a few typical Thoreauvian expressions in it that would let you know he wrote it even if his name were not on the title page. He writes: "The autumnal change of our woods has not made a deep impression on our own literature yet. October has hardly tinged our poetry."

And, after giving a scientific explanation of the reason for the fall change in leaf color, he says, "But I am more interested in the rosy cheek than to know what particular diet the maiden fed on." Or again: "October is the month for painted leaves. Their rich glow flashes round the world. As fruits and leaves and the day itself acquire a bright tint just before they fall, so the year is near its setting. October is the sunset sky; November the later twilight."

A week or so ago I mailed a fat envelope to a friend in England. If the Customs authorities there open it, as perhaps containing contraband, they will be startled by a shower of red and yellow and purple leaves gathered from New England's autumn as a gift to old England.

The Evening of the Years

Looking out of my bedroom window this morning, I noticed a tree still clothed in orange though all those around it were bare. It was beyond the far corner of the pasture in a rough growth of wild land where years ago I had tumbled a barrage of boulders bulldozed from the field. I made a mental note to check on it after breakfast.

This is the first day of November. There was white frost on the ground earlier, although the thermometer read thirty-nine degrees Fahrenheit. It was not freezing, though it seemed so. It was the sort of autumn day I wait all year to enjoy. We do not get many such, though we are blessed with more than elsewhere in the country.

I shocked someone the other day by telling him that the two months in the year I like least are July and August. I meant it. There are several reasons—the main one, I guess, is that there are too many people around. In November they are gone, and there is rarely fog, and the temperature is perfect. Furthermore, the garden does not need much attention, just a little grass cutting and all the pleasant autumn jobs gardeners enjoy: digging and storing beets and carrots, gathering in the leeks (mine are as big or bigger than the one displayed by Jim Crockett in his book), digging a few parsley plants to carry on for a while in the kitchen or greenhouse, cutting down the asparagus and covering it with rockweed, burning weeds and trash.

I know one is not supposed to burn garden trash. The compost heap is the place for it and is where most of it goes, but I always save a little out to burn—and justify my action by adding a few roots of witch grass to offer up as a sacrifice to the gods of the garden. When I was a child, we always had a garden bonfire in the fall. Our old gardener carefully saved the witch grass roots to burn in it, claiming that it was the only way anybody could be sure that a root of witch grass was dead. Strange, but after all those many, many years a garden bonfire smells just the same. Old George, who has been dead now these fifty years and who taught me how to garden, comes to mind again with the first whiff of the acrid smoke from the fire. I can remember dodging around it with my eyes streaming, trying to keep to windward and never succeeding for very long. I still can't. When it was turned to a pile of white ashes, a shovelful of soft earth was spread on it to make sure it would not blaze up during the night under the caress of a vagrant puff of wind. Afterward, when I ran out of the cold November twilight into the warmth of the kitchen, my grandmother would say, "My, how you do smell. Now you go right up and wash and change your clothes before tea time."

Kitchen garden bonfires and the fragrance of chrysanthemums spell autumn to me. I haven't had my fire yet, but I have smelled the mums. Even though they never got transplanted from the vegetable garden (where I grow them until fall) into the front flower beds, they have not suffered. I have not been able to do quite so many things this year as in the past, but the chrysanthemums have not failed me even though they did not get the pinching and feeding they usually enjoy. I bought fifty or so rooted cuttings in the spring, and they are now all in bloom, fine large plants in a multitude of varieties. Rooted cuttings are the only way to buy chrysanthemums. Plant them in the spring, pinch them and feed them, and they will bless you with a world of color in October and November. A little frost will not harm them, and their cost will not hurt your pocketbook. You can buy ten cuttings in the spring for what a single flowering plant will cost you in the fall.

A lot of things are still blooming on this first day of November. Besides the chrysanthemums, which are at their best, there are many less spectacular holdouts against winter. There are, of course, the fall crocus under their bed of periwinkle, but they are to be expected, for this is their season. A little unexpected are the California poppies. There are two beds of them against the outside greenhouse wall. Their flowers seem to be an even deeper orange than during the summer, and if picked just as the pointed bud splits, they will last for a long time indoors. There are a few gladiolus, small bulbs that did not come along as fast as the larger ones. Those I have are all a deep purple. The anemone, not *A. japonica* but *A. vitifolia*, has a few flowers, and there are roses to be found here and there. Pansies, of course, lots of nicotiana, a couple of annual hollyhocks, and in a bed against the house are some sweet alyssum and a marigold or two.

The shrubs put on a good show in November. Several roses are loaded with orange hips. The rugosas are gone, eaten either by us or the birds, but an old-fashioned rose—*Rosa alba*—is weighed down with fruit. There are several euonymus with brilliant scarlet capsules that were filled with yellow seeds, making a brilliant contrast, but the birds have rifled them. Not spectacular, but fragrant and now in full bloom, are ten-foot bushes of autumn witch hazel. They are pleasant to cut and bring indoors, where they perfume a room.

It was afternoon before I found time to walk down through the pasture, but when I did, after climbing the gate, I discovered that the "orange" tree was a dead spruce literally covered with bittersweet. There were several plants, and I am of two minds about what to do. Bittersweet is lovely to look at but terribly invasive. I think I'll cut down half of them and take the berried branches indoors or give them to friends, but leave the roots. There will be more berries next year, but the plants won't spread as fast. I'll leave it to the next person who farms these acres to decide what to do.

The cold was getting into my bones as I walked back, for in November the sun has little warmth, but I noticed that the grass was short and springy like that on the English downs, which have been cropped by sheep for four hundred years. I made a note too that one of my sheep had a bloody ear and wondered if a dog had been at her. I shall have to get Ivar to catch her tomorrow so I can examine her more closely. I'm not much good at chasing sheep these days, and if I were able to catch one, I doubt I could turn her over. Nothing lasts forever.

The Weasel in Winter

One of the few things man has not been able to mess up is a storm. He has polluted the rivers and the lakes, burned the forests, torn the living skin from the land so that the soil blows away, even used the world's oceans as cesspools, but he has not been able to do a damned thing to control the wind and the rain and the snow, and please God he never will.

The gusts hit fifty knots around supper time yesterday, or at least that is the figure the man on television gave, and he had it from the Coast Guard weather station so it was probably correct. Right in the middle of it, just as the darkness deepened, I heard a dog barking. Happy was on the couch (and would have had better sense than to venture out into that sort of blow anyway) and Gay was asleep by the fire, so I put on some foul-weather gear and let myself out on the lee side of the house. We have one ewe left in the pasture, but she was not suffering; she was supplied with hay and had a shelter behind the spruces. I had chased a dog away a couple of times recently, however, and was concerned that it might have come back. A dog, even a gentle one, can go wrong on sheep.

It was quiet behind the house, but when I turned the corner the wind and rain, now driving in from the northeast, hit me solidly like a wall of water. I gasped and ducked back to consider the situation, then headed out on a starboard tack. Losing fifty feet to leeward in going fifty feet ahead, I fetched up in front of the henhouse door, which was where I wanted to be. Inside the barn, the sound of the wind was muffled, but the timbers creaked as they braced their century-old bones against the blow, one of many they must have braved over the years.

When I flipped the switch, the electric company was there, as they advertise on TV, and the hens began to complain about the light disturbing their rest. I was not concerned about them, though, so I walked on through the tie-up. Cleaning off a cobwebby window with an old grain sack, I shone my flashlight across the road. I could see no dog and at first could not see the ewe either, but by and by found her against the fence under a spruce, looking like one of the weathered granite boulders that dot the field. Closer, in the barnyard, the Highlanders were lying in their shelter and calmly chewing their cuds as though they were enjoying a siesta on a summer afternoon. Occasional scuds of rain blew in on them, but the cattle's long shaggy coats shed it easily. I suppose all it did was to remind them of their native western Scotland.

When I got back into the warmth of the kitchen, I could taste the salt on my lips. We are a hundred feet above mean low water and about eight hundred feet back from the shoreline, but in a heavy easterly gale the wind tears spray from the ragged waves and blows it across the pasture and over the road to whiten the windows of the house.

Helen asked, "Is everything all right?" I replied, "Yes. I think it will blow itself out by morning." It did, but the teeth of the storm gnashed all night long.

I used to wonder what happened to birds on such a night, but I have learned since that they take to the woods. I can throw a rock into the conifers south of the house and dislodge birds by the dozen after a storm.

Wildlife mortality goes up during hard winters, but it is the weaker ones that do not make it, and so nature culls the unfit. Our feathered friends, as the wild-bird-seed salesmen like to call them, are on the whole pretty tough. If they have any friendship for us, it is of the kind that my grandmother used to call "cupboard love," and if we were not around they would get along well enough. Rarely a winter passes that we do not have a resident robin somewhere around Amen Farm. Worms are hard to come by in January, but robins can make do with other food. I have seen them pecking at rotten wild apples, and they eat berries, beetles, and grubs even when worms are available during the summer.

There is a surprising amount of wildlife visible in the winter that blends into the background in the summer. Driving one evening in the dark of night, I caught sight of a movement ahead of us. As I watched, a weasel, whiter than the snowbanks but for the tip of its tail, snaked swiftly across the road. It was intent upon its business and wasted no time crossing the highway. It hurried not because of me but because it was hot on a scent. Weasels hunt with their nose and move astonishingly fast in spite of their short legs. They are not to be diverted by such unimportant obstructions as automobiles or humans. I was once standing beside a stone wall at Amen Farm, watching for a chipmunk I had just seen dive between the stones, when a weasel, obviously in pursuit, ran headlong over the toe of my boot, taking no more notice of me than if I had been a log of wood.

Most people have never seen a weasel, but they and numberless other wildlings go about their daily lives as if we did not exist. They live unseen among us in much greater numbers than we suspect. Although I have spent a large part of my life in the country, I cannot honestly say that I have seen more than a dozen weasels. They are abundant, though, as trappers will affirm.

When I was a child, gamekeepers in England hated weasels and nailed their skins on barn doors along with other "vermin." I also knew a few less law-abiding characters who used ferrets (semi-tame weasels) to catch rabbits. The method was to stake nets over the holes in a rabbit warren and then slip a ferret into one of the holes. The rabbits, who are terrified of weasels (and with good reason), bolt into the nets in their panic to escape. The poachers usually got back their ferrets, but occasionally when a rabbit was not fast enough off the mark, a ferret would catch one underground. In that event, the ferret could usually be chalked off as lost, as it would not emerge until it had finished with the rabbit. As I remember them, ferrets were yellowish-white, while our North American weasels are brown with a yellowish-white underbody, except in winter, when they turn white all over except for the black tail tip.

Whenever I look at a snowbank now, and we have quite a few from January to March, I am reminded of the weasel that darted across my path. It occurs to me that for all our modern scientific wisdom, were anything to hiccough in our computerized society, nature, which stands ever waiting, would flow over us and submerge us without a trace.

Relax and Enjoy It

Christmas, like so much else worthwhile, sometimes gets buried beneath its trappings. Make no mistake about it, though; it is there for those who seek it. It is, I think, what William Wordsworth described as "central peace subsisting at the heart of endless agitation." It lives not in the "Silent Nights" that blare neither silent nor holy from every shopping center, but in that small inward sanctuary of the mind where all things fine and precious have their being.

My own earliest Christmas memory, unaided by any record, is of being hoisted into the air, giggling and screaming, by my brother, and somehow wriggling loose so that in my descent I bloodied his nose. I cannot recollect when or where it happened or what the outcome of my misadventure was. First grief over the absence of a voice long loved but now forever gone is transmuted by the magic of Christmas into something bittersweet that, as the years fade, will retain only its sweetness.

One later Christmas holiday stands out above all others. I was returning home from boarding school for the first time alone. I was, I suppose, about nine or ten years old and just sufficiently apprehensive about the journey that it added a spice of adventure. I need have had no fear, for in those days everyone was a child's guardian. On boarding the train I was turned over to the guard, who I am sure had several other young charges. Occasionally in his passage he would stop and say a word. When we reached the town where I was to change trains, he relinquished me to a porter, who in turn sat me on a hard wooden seat and instructed me to stay there until he told me what to do. As several trains came and went, my concern mounted, but I stayed put. In those far-off days there were chocolate machines on the railway platforms that would dispense a small rectangle of hard chocolate for a penny. I had taken the precaution to arm myself with a pocketful of coins and must have played the "slot machine" a dozen times before my train came puffing in. Being a local, it arrived full of shoppers, and I was surrounded by people and packages. Not having far to go, I did not venture away from the door, but I need not have been concerned, for half a dozen people had learned of my destination and were ready to see that I disembarked at the right place.

I can remember standing alone on the platform with my bag, watching the train disappear down the track and seeing the other passengers leave until I was left by myself. I do not think I was worried; the surroundings were familiar, and in any event only a few minutes passed before I heard the wheels of a trap drawn by a fat middle-aged mare grind around a corner. My grandfather was at the reins. He greeted me with, "Well, boy, did you have a good trip?" and I answered, "Yes, sir." I had a very great respect for my grandfather and always addressed him as sir, as indeed I did all my male elders. I jumped into the back of the conveyance, and Grandfather picked up my bag and joined me, exhaling a faint fragrance of cigars and brandy that was as much a part of him as his voice and bearing. Without saying another word, he handed me the reins, and the horse, feeling his weight in the carriage, set off at a smart trot.

Never have I been happier. We had not far to go, but that ride remains in my memory as the most blissful experience I have ever had. It was a green Christmas and still warm enough for the countryside to be fragrant. The hedges were leafless, but here and there an evergreen enlivened the scene, and one could see out into the fields where a little color still showed beneath the dead stubble. I don't remember much else about that Christmas. The ride home behind the horse, who was more anxious to get to the stable than I was to complete my journey, made all else an anticlimax. I can still hear the clop, clop, clop of the mare's hooves on the graveled road and smell the odor of horse (something that most modern kids know little of) and remember how superior I felt to be sitting up high enough to look over the low hedges into the fields beyond.

Now I too am a grandfather and a great grandfather, and the long years stretch out behind me like the wake of a ship. What I have learned over those years is that material things are unimportant. What is remembered and distinctive is the *atmosphere* of Christmas, the spirit of goodwill and affection that prevails. I have memories of many Christmases past, but I cannot recall more than half a dozen things I received as gifts. On the other hand, I retain the warmest recollections, which never fade, of friends and events at the Christmas season—they never wear out, get lost, or are discarded.

We've strayed a long way from the old-fashioned Christmas. Even the exchanging of Christmas greetings is different. Originally Christmas greetings were just that, friends calling upon one another in person bearing small gifts for the children or a jar of jelly or some other item that was a family specialty. People visited the shut-ins, admired the Christmas trees, went caroling, and, since their circle of acquaintances was small, saw them all unless they lived "away."

Now the Christmas card has taken over. At its best it is a pleasant personal message to absent friends; at its worst it is a meaningless custom that enriches the card manufacturers and drives the postal authorities insane while it swells their coffers. Perhaps the high cost of postage will now result in people adding more than just their names to the printed message.

Last year a friend gave me a little stiff fourfold card, a calendar for the year 1888. It is decorated with pale yellow and lavender pansies, beloved of our Victorian ancestors, and breathes the simplicity of a less hurried age. It was the gift I enjoyed most. It cost my friend only a little in cash but it told me that I was in her thoughts, for she knew I would be entranced with it, and that is what Christmas is all about—thoughtfulness.

The human spirit seems to have unquenchable optimism despite continual ups and downs. For a good many years my childlike feeling of optimism about Christmas has carried me into the festivities, which always promise a great deal even though I am well aware that they usually leave me exhausted and disillusioned and temporarily bankrupt. The following year, when Christmas again approaches—singing her cheerful carols, displaying her charms, and exercising her seductions—I say to myself, "She is beautiful. I cannot reject her, but his time it will be different. I am wiser and more experienced. I shall be kind but I shall be firm." But then I embrace her. I press her to my bosom and have a high old time. All is joy to the world, and it is not until after Twelfth Night, when the pipers stop piping, that it dawns on me that I have been had again.

Now, lest you think me a crabbed old Scrooge, I should explain that I do not think my disappointment is because of any intrinsic fault in Christmas itself. I do not feel there is anything wrong with celebrating the birth of Christ. The difficulty lies in the fact that Christmas has been captured by bandits.

The idea of gathering family and friends together around the festive board, exchanging a few simple gifts, and enjoying the faces of small children looking up the chimney for Father Christmas or Santa Claus has nothing but good to recommend it. It is a fine custom that during at least one day in the year makes the meanest smile in spite of himself. It makes us realize that even under the most unlikely exterior most of us shelter a desire to let down our guard and accept everyone as a friend.

But during my lifetime I have watched Santa whip up his steeds to the point where we need a dual highway to prevent them from trampling on the Thanksgiving pumpkins. And as Christmas now merges with no more than a hiccough into New Year, all that is needed is a new holiday in January to carry us through without pause in one long buying bender until Saint Valentine gets in his licks in February. I think that many have come to realize that someone has made off with Christmas and left in its place a shoddy substitute. While I would not be so brash as to claim that there is a Christmas backlash, there *are* signs that a sizable group of concerned citizens are unhappy about Christmas having become a commercial rather than a family and religious festival. The affluent society is responsible for the falacious idea that Christmas can be bought and that happiness is an equation of wealth. They say, in effect, that if a ten-dollar present makes you happy, a hundred-dollar present will make you ten times more joyous, and if you were to be presented with a solid gold putter, as a friend of mine was (he keeps it in the safe), you would be deliriously happy. I have yet to be convinced that children are happier with a dozen gifts rather than two or three. They usually wind up playing with the shipping cartons anyway.

Here and there, by conviction or preference, there are increasing numbers of people who want to celebrate Christmas for its true worth, for its expression of peace to men of good will all over the earth, and its gifts of frankincense and myrrh that come from the heart and not the pocketbook—the gentle and kindly thought, the small and helpful remembrance, the telephone call or visit, the Christmas card with a few words of affection instead of the perfunctory coldness of a printed name.

Here, in the country, it's a little easier to catch the spirit of the season and hold its gift separate from its wrappings. Soon it will be Christmas Eve, the most magical night of the year, when, if you go into the barn at midnight, you will find the cows on their knees and a soft light like a new dawn reflected from the dusty windows. I know it is so because I took my grandchildren there one Christmas Eve. The snow was deep outside, but when we opened the door to the warmth of the tie-up, right at the stroke of midnight, old Cindy, our Guernsey, got up on her knees—we saw her. There was also a luminescent glow from the cobwebs over the stalls. The sophisticated ten-year-old said it was the reflection from my lantern—the littlest one and I knew better.

Home

Here is our home, here our country.
(Hic Domus, Haec Patria Est)

— Virgil, *Aeneid* VII, 19 B.C.

Things That Go Bump in the Night

Anyone who makes his home in the country soon learns to live with animals other than those of the human species. There are enough of the latter, but the ones I'm referring to are those which, with our usual modesty, we term subhuman. I don't mean dogs and cats and cows and sheep and pigs, or even hens and ducks and geese, for these have been domesticated so long that they are almost part of the human family. I mean the ones we call wild. Wild because we have been unable to seduce them from their independence with free food and lodging—not for very long anyway. After who knows how many years we have only just made it with the cat, and even sweet pussy is likely to vanish for a week or so now and then just to prove that she doesn't really need us. The "subhumans" I'm talking about go bump in the night, or rattle the garbage can lid, or disappear behind a rock, or evaporate into the woodland so that we do not know whether we really saw them or not. There are also the more intimate species that make no bones about living in our houses but are no more domestic than a seagull.

Having lived in old houses most of my life I am well acquainted with house dwellers. One of my previous abodes had a kitchen wing, added in the 1800s, where we did most of our living. One wall featured a good-sized brick fireplace with a Dutch oven behind an iron door. One evening as Helen and I were sitting in front of the fire enjoying our pre-dinner cocktail, a great commotion arose inside the Dutch oven. "Well," I said, "I guess we've got rats again." (In passing, I have to admit that we kept trash in the oven because it was good for nothing else.) I called our Scottie, who was death on rats. Helen stood on the loveseat, and I opened the oven door. Out fell two chimney swifts locked in mortal combat.

In this same kitchen we used to entertain guests by allowing them to watch Boxy, our six-toed Maine cat, catch mice. The walls were panelled with oak boards, and only the cat knew how many mice there were behind them. After dinner while we were having our coffee, the mice would perform for us. First one, then another would poke a whiskery nose up between the burners on the gas stove. Boxy would crouch motionless on the floor, four or five feet away. Pretty soon a mouse, emboldened by the quiet, would come out onto the top of the stove and hunt around for crumbs. Not until it was far enough from the burner holes that a safe retreat was impossible did the cat jump. When she did, she made the leap in one smooth motion and never missed.

The house had a wide brick terrace where we were accustomed to sit on summer evenings. We would stay there until the bats began to fly, at which point we would go in—not because we mind bats but because the bats and mosquitos arrived simultaneously. One evening I saw the flittermice emerging from under the bargeboard on the gable end of the roof. I had assumed that they lived in the barn, but apparently not, so a few days later I decided to have a look in the attic, which was separate from the rest of the house and accessible only through a trapdoor in the upper hall. I had never opened it before and never did again. There must have been a hundred bats, all hanging very tidily from the rafters like Monday morning's wash. We lived there together in the greatest harmony for many years. Strangely, I do not recall seeing a bat in the house more than a couple of times in all the years we lived there.

Shading the front of this house were two enormously old and decrepit sugar maples, and on the wall was a thick growth of ivy infested by English sparrows. They were both dirty and noisy, and it was my custom when I got home in the evening, weary from my labors, to sit on the terrace armed with a .22 rifle loaded with dust shot and pick off the sparrows. When I could no longer hit them I would conclude that either it was too dark or I had had my quota of cocktails and go in to dinner. My wife put an end to this exercise after I blew a hole in the window screen and smeared some shot across a bedroom ceiling.

The maples housed an assorted population. For several years a family of raccoons made their home there. The front door to their apartment was level with our bedroom window, and we surveyed each other warily, like a couple of New York City tenement dwellers looking across an alley. There were several families of gray squirrels in the upper levels, but the most awesome tenants were a pair of great horned owls.

Bubo virginianus, which is what the naturalists call the great horned owl, is a bird of more than modest proportions. I have never measured one, but my bird book records that it can have a wingspan of five feet, and I can believe it. Additionally, it utters the most blood-curdling shrieks and horrid gurglings. The first time I heard it I sat bolt upright in bed and was sure that someone was being murdered in our front field. The owls stayed with us for three years, and, although I always ducked, I got used to seing them glide soundlessly across the terrace in the half-light of evening. I once read in a book called *Concord River,* by William Brewster, a noted ornithologist, that if you stand in a field after dark and squeak like a mouse, any owls that are about will hover over you. I tried it, but nothing happened, and in retrospect I think it was just as well because if old *Bubo virginianus* had hovered over me with his Boeing 747 wingspread, I would probably have had a heart attack.

Just a little while before we left that house to live at Amen Farm, we had another visitor, one not usually numbered among household fauna. I was shaving one morning when Helen called from the other bathroom in the hall, saying, "Come here. An animal with beady eyes just looked around the door at me and then went into the bedroom."

"What sort of animal?" I shouted back. "What is it? A rat? A mouse? A squirrel? Ask him his name and tell him not to be looking at ladies in the bath."

"No, honest," she said. "I'm not kidding. I never saw one like this before."

When I went into the adjoining bedroom there was nothing in sight. I lifted the bed valance, and a lithe brown body shot out and jumped onto the window sill, whereupon I closed the window and caught it between the window and screen. It was a weasel.

I suppose that to the occupant of a high-rise apartment or a dweller in suburbia all this sounds pretty shocking, but it is a part of living in the country, and for some reason we found it amusing. Our fellow tenants attended to their business and we to ours, and if our paths crossed occasionally, we all pretended to be invisible.

Our daughter said the other day, "You must attract things." She had been sitting on the terrace when a five-foot black snake slithered gracefully across the stone floor in front of her. I looked at the snake and thought, maybe we do, maybe we do.

Old Houses

All my life, except for one period of about twenty years, I have been fortunate enough to live in old houses. I suppose most people today, when statistics tell us that families move an average of once every three years, would not consider an old house much of a blessing. They prefer them new and shiny, with all the latest gadgets built in, and foremost in their minds when they buy a house is how much profit they can make on it when it is sold. To an earlier generation, especially if they lived in the country, the idea of a new house had no enticement. The most desirable thing to fall to one's lot was to continue to occupy the house one was born in. If that did not transpire, one usually rented (or bought, if one could afford it) a house that had been previously occupied. There was then a continuity of life that has in these latter days escaped us, and old houses provided visible evidence of the unseen presence of one's predecessors.

I do not remember the house I was born in because I left it as an infant, but my grandmother's house, which I always think of as home because of childhood memories, was a very old English dwelling. No one knew exactly how old, but part of it was Elizabethan and some perhaps of even earlier vintage. It is hard to specifically date old houses because, as generations pass, each owner in turn adds or subtracts or modifies to suit current fashion or convenience. Our house had been in the family for a couple of hundred years, so there was convincing evidence, by document and word of mouth, for that length of time. But before our occupancy, only mossy stones all askew in the local churchyard recited the names connected with it.

My twenty-year occupancy of a new house was in one I had built for me in Pennsylvania. It was a pretty house, and I tried to make it look as old as I could by copying the lovely stone architecture of the southern part of the state, but it never felt old. Houses have to be long inhabited to capture the feeling of earlier times.

My next home—and I use the word advisedly, since many houses are not homes—was a large, white-painted brick, tidewater-style building on a hill overlooking Northbrook Village in Chester County, Pennsylvania. By American standards it was a very old house, having been built in 1726. The original owners and builders did not occupy it very long, but the family that followed them stayed on into the twentieth century—a matter of almost two hundred years. One day while I was digging in the garden I turned up a sleigh bell with the initial B on it. It had belonged to one of the Bakers, the long-time owners. I also found a beautifully finished white flint arrowhead, the kind that Indians used for bird shooting, which had been owned by even earlier residents of the neighborhood.

Close by the west side of the house was a depression that could be followed over the rolling, hilly country to the Brandywine River. It had once been a road over which British troops had marched to outflank Washington's army at the Battle of the Brandywine. Old houses accumulate stories as rocks do lichens, and one about "Whitehorn" (for that was the name of the house) was that these same troops had raided the springhouse, where the week's baking was set to cool, and made off with the pies. It has a ring of truth about it, for I have been a soldier and am acquainted with the habits of the military.

When I came to live in Maine I reluctantly sold "Whitehorn," but upon the encouragement of my daughter went back after a while and bought an even older house to occupy in spring and fall, much as people use property here in Maine for the summer. The house was quite small, just one room upstairs and one down, plus a kitchen. It stood on a hill and commanded long views over peaceful farmland. We thought it was a frame house when we bought it, but when we began to restore it, we found it was made of chestnut logs so hard that a nail could not be driven into them. The dating was not very exact, but with the help of the local historical society we found some authority for believing that it was built about 1700. It was a comfortable and protective house. I used to lie in bed, sheltered behind those log walls, and listen to the wind volleying over Thunder Hill, crying through the shelter belt, and fingering the window shutters; it reminded me of earlier days when all the surrounding country was forest inhabited by the Lani-Lenape Indians. We did not own this house for long, as I soon discovered that a man can no more have two houses than he can two wives.

Thirty years ago I found myself with another old house—not old by comparison with my previous homes but just graying a bit around the temples. As nearly as we can tell, Amen Farm (as we call it, though to the locals it is still remembered as the old Bowden place) was built in 1852. The oldest portion is a Cape Cod sort of structure to which was added at a later date two other houses, or parts of houses. The whole building was attached at some time, in line with typical New England continuous architecture, to a barn that is in itself made up of two sections. I suppose the first barn was erected when the oldest part of the house was built and the addition (a completely different type of construction) was hauled over and tied on later. Old houses grow by a process of gravitational accretion, the larger body attracting the smaller.

When we bought the place we continued in tradition by giving back to the old folks from whom we had purchased it the end section of the house, where they were living. It was between the part we wanted and the barn. They just cut it off, loaded it on a huge flatbed trailer, hauled it about a mile down the road, and set it on a new foundation. The neighbors, who liked to tease my namesake, Roy Bowden, alleged that he never even got out of bed during the journey. Be that as it may, I can testify that everything else was moved *in situ*—the furniture remained in place, the dishes in the closets, and the pots on the walls—and the Bowdens lived there for many more years.

Like the hill country in New Hampshire and Vermont, coastal Maine never has been true farmland. The inhabitants turned to the sea, but had enough cleared land to allow for a little subsistence farming. Though now overgrown and disappearing into puckerbrush and alder, rock walls bear witness to the outlines of onetime hayfields and rocky pastures. Most of the land comprised woodlots then and now.

Evidence of the old life lives on in my sway-roofed double barn. When I bought it there were stalls for a couple of work horses, lighted by the usual small, square windows covered with cobwebs. These stalls I later turned into tie-ups for a few Guernseys. When I would go to the barn to shake down a little hay, I'd hang my lantern on a grooved peg that had served previous owners as they milked in the early darkness of winter afternoons. The heavy plank floors are worn by the hooves of animals so that the harder knots project like small cobblestones, and the posts are polished smooth where horses and cattle have rubbed against them.

Just off the back of my hayfield, a few hundred feet into the woods, is a dug well. It is a good one, and the water is never more than a few feet below the surface of the ground. I wondered what a well was doing back in the woods until one day Lena told me that those woods had once been a pasture. The land was too full of boulders (it still is) to do anything with, so after the trees had been cut for pulp and cordwood the animals were turned in there to make "half a living" nibbling around the rocks. The well provided water, and Roy told me he used it to wash down the "hosses."

There were three families living here at one time, one in Lena's and

Roy's quarters and two in the part we kept. When we came here there was a double front door and twin staircases. Lena's end had a separate entrance. There were also a number of disintegrating henhouses, store-rooms, and implement sheds, plus another barn in a sad state of advanced disrepair. One dull autumn day, with a smoky southwester trailing its rainskirts across the land, we notified the fire company and had a grand conflagration. When the smoke finally cleared away, all that remained were the double house and the double barn.

We have made our own additions and changes, and I hope that those who come after us—for we are but brief tenants of this world—will want to both keep the best of the old and make their own contributions. New houses may be necessary, but I trust and hope that some of the young people I see breathing life into old farms and houses will be able to "hack it." The previous owners will, I am sure, be there in spirit to encourage them.

To Live Forever

I suppose that after the Taj Mahal and Cheops' pyramid were built nobody added anything to them because they were memorials to the dead. That is not true, however, of houses in which people live. Successive generations of politicians have felt the need of adding to the White House ever since the British set fire to it during the War of 1812, and most houses we ordinary mortals live in today have been added to or subtracted from to suit the needs or whims of current owners. I guess that if you took a hammer and a handful of nails to one of these modern glue and plywood houses it would collapse, but most old houses— more substantially built—have had a facelift somewhere along the line, or perhaps only the outhouse got moved indoors as people got more sophisticated.

All the houses I have ever lived in have had a working over. One old house in Pennsylvania, built in 1726, was changed in 1820 from a gable-roofed Georgian farmhouse into a large, square, three-story tide-water mansion with a new kitchen wing. I added my contribution by building a wide brick terrace around it. If the original owner/builder had been able to see it, he would not have recognized it.

The house I live in now has been altered a bit too. I have done a lot, but changes were made long before I bought it. It is separated from the barn now by a space of about fifty feet. When I took ownership, house and barn were joined—all but the ten feet spanned by a covered walkway, a sort of Bridge of Sighs, that old Roy Bowden used on snowy nights to avoid the winter blasts. The other forty feet were occupied by a piece of architecture built much later than the original house, which someone had hauled in and placed between the house and the barn. Its gable ran the wrong way and there was too much house for us anyway, so I told Roy he could have it if he would haul it off.

After we patched up and rebuilt such of the place as was left, I decided I would have been ahead of the game if I had put a match to it and built a new house across the road, but I didn't discover that until I had spent so much money that I couldn't afford to. Anyway, over a score of years we have added and subtracted, and now, when we are too old to do much more, we find that we are very happy with it—which is a very good thing because we don't have enough money to go to Florida or Nevada or California, where most old folks are heading these days.

We did one smart thing in the beginning: we hired a good architect. I have rebuilt half a dozen old houses (I hate new houses) and have learned to appreciate the value of an architect. You may have the ideas, but you need a professional to put them into being. Of course, you want to get a good architect—and there are bad architects, just as there are bad doctors and bad lawyers. But to find out if you have the sort of architect you want, you can go around and look at some of the houses he has designed and ask the owners what they think of them and if they are satisfied. Bad doctors bury their mistakes, and bad lawyers' unfortunate clients lose and go broke or to jail, but an architect's mistakes live on to shame him unless the owners are so discontented that they set fire to them.

Architect or not, good or bad, you cannot tell if a house exactly suits you until you live in it a while. As my wife says, you never know what a spouse is like until you live with him (or her), which is a little late to learn what doesn't suit you. Fortunately, with houses you can amend them, which is just about impossible with a wife or husband. Of course you can get a divorce, just as you can burn down your unsatisfactory house, but either is an expensive solution.

If you buy an old house and set about reforming it, you are quite apt to find that what you do leads to other changes or additions that had never occurred to you originally. You may also wind up with a real bonus. We did, when we decided it would be pleasant to have a front porch, or piazza, or whatever you choose to call an outside sitting space with a roof over it. Many old Maine houses have one but ours did not, so Bob, our architect, planned one for us. We enjoyed it for several years, but in the course of time it was borne in upon us that coastal Maine is not the place to bask in the open air, except perhaps on the Fourth of July. Accordingly, we closed in the porch with three large thermopane windows, which we justified buying by saying that they cost less than the winters in Florida all our friends seem to afford. Furthering the "old plantation" ambience, we bought a half dozen camellias for a couple of dollars apiece. They are now six feet tall and would be taller if I didn't prune them mercilessly every year.

I knew an old lady who planned to live forever by always having a building project on hand to keep her lively. She made it to ninety-six, which is not forever but is about as long as most of us want to hang around. I don't know what my next project is going to be, but as I expect to at least equal my grandmother, who shed herself of this world's cares at ninety-seven, I have time to think about it.

Frogs, Toads, and Icehouses

We have our share of frogs and toads in Maine, and I suppose newts and lizards, although I have never seen any of the latter. Where I once lived, near Lincolnville, I could always find a few salamanders by turning over a pile of rotting boards behind the icehouse. I used them for live bait when I could not get anything to rise to a fly. I hasten to add that there were no trout in the lake, just bass, yellow and white perch, and pickerel. The salamanders that inhabited my icehouse were such inoffensive little things that I felt bad about fishing with them, but they did not suffer long as they seemed fatally attractive to bass. One would hardly hit the water before there would be a swirl, and a bass, feeling the hook, would erupt from the surface like a rocket. We are all in the food chain, I would think—the bass eat the salamanders and I eat the bass.

Back in 1943, when I first went to summer on Lake Megunticook, almost everyone had an icehouse as part of their establishment. A few of the more modern folk changed to mechanical refrigeration when bottled gas came in, but most of us stuck with our icehouses. The ice was handy by, and as I remember it, Jake filled my icehouse sometime during the winter for eighteen dollars. It was good ice too, clear and hard, and lasted through Labor Day, although by that time you had to rummage around in the sawdust to find any, the large chunks that had gone into the icehouse in January having shrunk to pieces about the size of a Methodist hymnbook.

I sold the place in 1955, and by that time I too had bought a bottled-gas refrigerator. I didn't do it willingly. What happened was that old Jake, and old Jake's old horse, went through the ice twice in one winter. Jake said that he didn't mind taking a ducking once a year, he considered that more or less of an occupational hazard, but twice at his age was too much. Jake was in his seventies, and I guess his horse was the equine equivalent of a septuagenarian too, so he—they—both of them had a point. Anyway, they went out of the ice business, and as there was no electricity on the island I had no choice but to turn to what nowadays is called fossil fuel.

I guess brighter men than I understand how you make ice by lighting a little gas burner about as big as the pilot light on a stove, but it was a mystery to me—and one I was not really much interested in solving. I could understand ice out of the pond. Along about midwinter, when the thermometer dropped below zero and the ice was a foot thick, blocks were sawn out and hauled into the icehouse. All it cost was the labor, and there was no depletion of natural resources. I can confirm it because I am now older than Jake was then, and there is still just as much ice as ever despite all the martinis it has cooled for me and others over the years. I drove by the lake a couple of winters ago, and there she was, solid ice as far as I could see, with whirls of snow eddying like miniature tornadoes running ahead of the wind.

Some of the effete mainlanders bought electric refrigerators when the power company offered to run a line to the lake if enough would sign up, and enough did. I am glad that I was saved the necessity of making that decision, for pretty soon, in addition to refrigerators, they had electric lights and oil burners and baseboard heat and—God forgive them—telephones and television sets. On the island, when we wanted heat we lit the kitchen range and threw a couple of logs in the big open fireplace, and for light we basked in the warmth of a Coleman lamp. One of the best things about oil lamps is that they get you to bed on time. The combination of gradually dimming light as the chimney smokes up and the heat (which is a fringe benefit) usually overcomes the most gripping whodunit.

It is amazing how much hot water you can get out of a wood range. Rigged on the wall next to the stove we had a vertical forty-gallon copper tank that provided water for showers, dishwashing, and so on. It was a magnificent gleaming copper cylinder that glowed in the lamplight. It would have been more efficient—and would have saved some burned hands, no doubt—if it had been covered with insulation, but to do so would have been sacrilege. Anyway, we had all the wood we wanted, so efficiency was of no moment, and people did not put their hands on the tank more than once.

The shower was a bit tricky. In the middle of the stall, directly overhead, was a device that resembled the sprinkler of a giant watering can. For it to work, the faucets had to be in the fully open position; otherwise, the water merely dribbled out around the edges. The pressure was provided by a gravity tank on the roof. After a couple of episodes when the water failed in the middle of a bath, I learned to check the level of water in the tank before I disrobed. As there was no mixing valve, just separate controls, getting the hot and cold water to commingle, as the lawyers say, made bathing a hazardous enterprise. Of course, if anyone opened a faucet elsewhere in the house, all bets were off. I can still hear in memory the anguished screams of a lady or the profanity of a man when the water suddenly turned to ice or steam just about the time the victim was properly lathered up.

Somehow I have gotten afield from frogs and toads and don't quite know how to find my way back except to say that our rainy weather is heaven to slugs and that the natural enemy of a slug is a toad and that I saw one this morning. As a child I was warned never, under any circumstances, to harm a toad. If by chance I discovered one in my wanderings, I was to carefully carry it home and deposit it tenderly somewhere in the shade of the garden. They say that in France selling toads for the protection of gardens is universal. Now, if you have an old icehouse that provides a safe, damp retreat, you may find a toad there and so won't have to go to France to buy one. I have no doubt but that it won't be long before there'll be a market for toads in America, just as there is for ladybugs, which are sold by the pound to environmentally motivated gardeners who aim to keep the pests in their gardens to a minimum using nature's own remedy.

A Little Larceny

When I let Happy and Gay out for their pre-bedtime run last night a thin snow was falling. It was not the first of the season, for we have had several flurries in the past few weeks, but the weather bureau had been softening us up for a severe winter storm, and this was apparently the start of it. The dogs did not stay out long. Happy, who is the elder, powdered her nose and returned at once. Even Gay, who loves to run, made but a few quick circuits of the dooryard before she too barked to come in.

Indoors it was bright and cozy. Outside it was dark and cold. Even had it not been snowing the only lights I could have seen would be those of the lighthouses on Green Island and Bass Harbor Point, but with the snow drifting down I looked out into a gray world. I suppose that to someone accustomed to living where friendly lights in neighboring houses and the headlights of passing traffic are a way of life, this silent darkness would have seemed menacing—but to us it is like being wrapped in a soft, protective cocoon.

We do not have *all* our preparations for winter accomplished yet but are well on the way. We try as a rule to be snugged down for hard weather by early December; usually any blow prior to that time is just in the way of a preliminary bout. The storm sashes have been hung and the outside of the windows cleaned for the last time until spring. The oil tank has been filled and extra gasoline for the emergency generator cached down by the barn. The heating pan to keep the hens' water from freezing has been connected, and we hope that the hens are by now all grown sensible enough to deposit their eggs in the nest boxes and not on the floor. Hens keep themselves comfortable enough at night on their roost, but eggs laid on the floor freeze.

As a child I grew up in the country and took pleasure then (I had a little larceny in my mind) in the apples and potatoes in the cold cellar and the orderly rows of preserves and canned vegetables on the shelves. I still do today, although now I have to open the door of the freezer to see most of our winter supply. Potatoes and beets and carrots and a few apples we still store in the cellar, the beets and carrots in sand, but I think that frozen peas and beans and corn are superior to those canned or dried—although we still, of course, dry our Saturday night beans. Onions and shallots and winter squash we keep on the attic floor. I guess it is the squirrel in me, but I find myself opening the freezer door as I pass by just so I can admire the plenty that the land and a little work have blessed us with.

This is an oldish house, old for Maine anyway. It was in such sad shape when we bought it that we had, for all practical purposes, to rebuild it. It had never had central heat or inside toilets or water or electricity, so when we put them in we rearranged the inside of the house a bit. We wound up with three fireplaces: one in the little study where I am typing, one in the living room, and another in the dining room. The last one is largely ornamental because the room is small and the person sitting back to the fire gets roasted. The other fireplaces we use pretty constantly, and we cut a few cords of wood each winter to supply them.

Cordwood is another emotional plus. It is stacked neatly in the barn with a pile of kindling beside it, and every time I pass by I have a feeling of comfort and assurance—I want to pat it. The oil tank is underground, and while its contents contribute most to keeping us warm, they don't do anything for me psychically. I have a neighbor living up the road a piece who has the neatest woodpile for miles around. He has some wood in his shed but most of it is stacked with geometrical exactness in his dooryard. I think he must put a square on the pile, for not one stick projects an inch beyond its neighbor. He has a lot of wood too, because it is his only fuel. Every time I drive to the village and pass his house a little bell of pleasure rings in my mind.

One would think that with all the food we have on hand we would buy nothing all winter—and in fact we seldom do, but for scallops and smelts, which are winter provender. When the inshore lobstermen haul their traps for the last time about November first (an unregulated but generally accepted changeover date) the scallop draggers take over. Except for a gallon or so that we carry over for a few weeks at the end of the season, we never eat frozen scallops. If we want scallops we buy them from our next-door neighbor, who will stop on his way home and dip us out a quart or so. I sometimes go to the harbor to get them from the boats, but Helen discourages me, saying that I eat too many raw on my way home. I don't dispute her.

Smelts we buy, starting in December, from a little store in the neighboring village of Surry. As soon as the cold has been around long enough the smelt fishermen push their tents out onto the ice of the cove, and when I see them I begin to watch for a sign saying "Fresh Surry Smelts," hanging next to the gas pump in front of the store. It is only a small sign and is never out very long, for there is no big harvest of smelts. Last winter was, for some reason unknown, a bad one, and I had smelts only twice. This year I hope will be better, for fresh Surry smelts fried crisp and brown can never be enjoyed except by those who live here. Like a fine *vin du pays,* they do not travel and will spoil with age.

I find nothing to complain of in winter.

Winter Fare

Like all who live in the country, I am constantly asked by summer visitors what I do in the winter. I usually give them some noncommittal answer and do not tell them that if it were not for the winter, February in particular, I could hardly bear living where I do. There seems to be a generally held opinion that out here, beyond the sidewalk's end, we hibernate after we get the summer cottages closed and our pulse rate does not speed up until they are opened again in the spring.

I do not mean that we do not enjoy July and August, for that is all the summer we get in Maine, but fall and spring are infinitely preferable, and winter has a quality of domesticity and neighborliness that is less felt during the rest of the year.

February is usually filled with sunshine, interrupted only by an occasional snowstorm that serves to keep the fields and gardens white and protected. When the sun is shining on the snow, there is not a crevice in the house where a spider could hide unobserved. But the winter afternoons close in early and afford an opportunity for a book by the fireside, a blessing not available to most apartment dwellers.

Recalling a Quaker rhyme about the second month, from the days when I lived among them in Pennsylvania, I checked my memory in Bartlett and found it and some other tags. The Quaker one goes:

> *Fourth, eleventh, ninth and sixth*
> *Thirty days to each affix:*
> *Every other thirty-one*
> *Except the second month alone.*

The New England version is:

> *Thirty days hath September,*
> *April, June and November:*
> *All the rest have thirty-one*
> *Excepting February alone*
> *Which hath but twenty-eight, in fine*
> *Till leap year gives it twenty-nine.*

I had not realized that these familiar mnemonics were in use as long ago as 1606, but one is given from "The Return from Parnassus," which sings:

> *Thirty days hath September*
> *April, June and November.*
> *February hath twenty-eight alone:*
> *All the rest have thirty-one*
> *Excepting leap year—that's the time*
> *When February's days are twenty-nine.*

All of these poetasters had trouble with "one" and "alone." You have to make up your mind to say either "twenty-eight alun" to rhyme with thirty-one, or "thirty-own" to rhyme with alone.

Not many of us remember that Julius Caesar, in addition to making the lives of innumerable schoolboys miserable with *"Gallia omnia est divisia en partes tres,*" was responsible for leap year. Along with the head of his Department of Scientific Research, a man named Sosigenes, he fixed the mean length of the year at 365 1/2 days and added an extra one every four years in order to gladden the hearts of the spinsters and make things come out even.

They missed it by a hair, though, because in order to keep the stars in their courses leap year has to be omitted every four thousand years. However, as I do not expect to be around (and if mankind does not mind its ways, none of our descendants will be witnesses either), I do not intend to distress myself over this small celestial miscalculation.

One thing that really annoys me about the monkeying around with the calendar that has been going on over the years is that the English, having held out until 1752, failed to exhibit their usual stubbornness and surrendered to the Papists. Up to that time they had observed the New Year on March 25. From then on they followed the example of the rest of Europe and used January 1, which is the silliest thing I know. March 25 is pretty close to the vernal equinox, whereas January 1 is slap in the middle of winter and is remarkable for nothing except hangovers and unpaid Christmas bills.

While here on the coast of Maine there is not much life in the garden in February—except for the deer that nibble back the new growth on the ornamental junipers and crabapples (they never touch the wild ones) and the mice who busy themselves devouring the crocus and tulip bulbs—there are other pleasures. One of the nonvegetarian gustatory delights available in winter, and one that the summer visitor never experiences, is fresh scallops. True, they may be had frozen in July and August, but no one who has ever tasted fresh ones, icy cold and a couple of hours out of salt water, equates one type with the other. We freeze some toward the end of the season but soon eat them, for they quickly lose their distinctive qualities—delicate tenderness and elusive flavor. They are like the wine that should be drunk with them— Muscadet, which is best the year following the vintage and over the hill in a couple more.

When I want scallops I bundle up and go down to the little harbor at Naskeag Point, where the scallopers row ashore from the draggers in the early darkness of a winter afternoon. My friend Lawrence, hipbooted and oilskinned, dips me a quart from the big, clean galvanized garbage can they have been shucked into. I put my mason jar on the seat beside me and eat them like peanuts as I drive home. To my mind they are never as tasty as when they are raw and just out of the nearly freezing waters of the bay.

They are not "bay scallops" in the sense of being small, although they are dragged from the bottom of Blue Hill Bay. They are full-sized, and if you want them smaller, you can cut them up. I have eaten the small bay scallop and can assure you that it is not in any respect better than ours, and you need more to make a meal.

We eat scallops raw, sautéed, stewed, as Coquille St. Jacques (with cream and mushrooms, or wine and garlic), or in any other way that circumstances and available additions make possible. When all is said and done, though, I like them best raw, although I might not if I had to buy them in the market. If they are to be cooked, my favorite recipe, a simple one, is to sauté however many scallops are needed in a little butter until they turn white on the inside and are golden on the outside. We usually serve them with a mixture of tomatoes, onions, and peppers that we cook and freeze from time to time in the summer.

Some people serve them with cocktails, skewered on toothpicks and marinated in lime or lemon juice. I think that is gilding the lily. Besides, it makes me cringe to see them, for they are live, like oysters or clams, and when the citric acid hits them they flinch in the dish and turn white.

Another February blessing is the saltwater smelt. It too is not available until after the summer hordes have departed, which is a very good thing as they would drive up the price and diminish the supply for us winter denizens of the frozen north. Our local supply comes from where a little river tumbles down from a pond into the bay at Surry (which is not the way the English spell it, but our ancestors were ear-rather than eye-minded spellers).

Smelt fishing is a combination of pleasure and profit, with a heavy accent on the former. For those who are unfamiliar with the art, it should be explained that a smelt tent is a small house, big enough to hold two people, a stove, and a bottle of whiskey. The tent is made of canvas stretched over a light wooden frame. Beside the door, which is just large enough to pass through comfortably, is a window about a foot square that lights the interior sufficiently to permit the fishermen to ply their craft. On one wall is a bench, and in front of it is a rectangular hole cut in the ice. Overhead is a rack from which the lines descend through the ice to where, it is hoped, the smelts are doing whatever it is smelts do in February.

People invariably ask if it is not a cold job. It is not, and anyone who has sat in a smelt tent will so certify. As a matter of fact, the fug can get pretty thick when a couple of pipes are going and the stove is smoking. The stoves are homemade. They operate on the principle of a pot burner and generate quite a lot of heat. If by chance your feet should get cold, a small sip of bourbon seems to descend to the proper place and take care of things.

Surry is a pretty village that is all uphill—or downhill, depending upon your direction of travel—and boasts perhaps a couple of dozen houses on the main road, plus two country stores (*real* country stores where people buy food or things to use, not to hang on the wall or give away). If you keep your eyes peeled you will see small signs reading "Surry Smelts" hanging outside their doors when the smelts are running.

I never go through Surry on my various business affairs during winter without watching for the signs. If they are out blowing in the wind, I rarely pass without stopping to buy a couple of pounds. Whatever we were going to have for dinner goes back into the refrigerator and we feast on smelts. If dinner is too far advanced to be put aside, they are fine fare for breakfast or lunch. As is true of scallops, the best way to cook smelts is the simplest. If you are fussy, like my wife, you remove the head and tail before placing them in the pan, and filet them, removing the backbone, after they are on your plate. Most of us, however, just fry the whole fish (they are best about six inches long) and eat it all. Cooked in butter, but not overcooked, they are golden and delectable. Some cooks prefer to start with a little bacon to provide the fat, as they would when cooking lake trout. I'll be happy either way just as long as I can get the smelts.

Somehow or other we manage to tough it out Down East here in the winter with our Coquille St. Jacques and lobster thermidor and fried smelts. When you are shivering in your fireless apartments, just think of us throwing a couple more birch logs (one dollar each in town) on the blazing hearth and finishing up the bourbon left over from the last smelting expedition.

Friendly Natives

I have heard it said that New Englanders are reserved and difficult to know, that they are unfriendly and unresponsive and that you may live with them for months or years and get no more than a cursory "good day." That may be, but I get a lot of letters from people who think they'd be happier here than where they are. Such letters usually cause me to look back and read the particular column referred to in the letter to see what might have sparked their desire. One was about driving on a foggy night. Fog is about the same no matter where you are. The world closes in around you, and for a while your concerns are bounded by a circle ten feet in diameter. You stop worrying about nuclear bombs, the condition of the stock market, or quarrels in the Near East (which, after all, date back to Biblical days). Your immediate and overriding concern is whether you can find your way home without winding up in the ditch. Maybe it is the immediacy of rural life that attracts those not living it.

I sometimes think that one of the healthiest things about living in the country is the concern one has with daily matters. International problems over which we have no control assume their proper proportions.

In the country your garbage does not just disappear as it does in the city (at least, you hopes it does) when you drop it down the incinerator shaft or put it out with the rubbish. Country dwellers must lug it off to the town dump or bury it somewhere on the back forty or make compost of it.

Your water (pure, you hope, but at least free from chlorine) comes out of your well—if it does not run dry or if the electricity does not fail in a storm. When it does, you wait a while until the utility company crew gets around in the worst of weather to make repairs. For obvious reasons, failures usually occur in bad weather.

If there is what insurance companies call an "unfriendly fire," you get busy and try to put it out, meanwhile calling for your neighbors to give a hand—and they do, quickly too. And the volunteer fire department comes as soon as possible, but you are your own first line of defense.

I guess people want their children to grow up in an atmosphere where the emphasis is on people instead of things. Maybe the clue is in my friend's question, "Have you found Utopia?" I haven't located Utopia, for it is the soul of men's desiring and so can only exist in the mind. Sir Thomas More knew this when he coined the word four hundred years ago out of two Greek words meaning "not anywhere."

It is far more important and necessary to be able to put up with your neighbor in the country than it is in the city even though there are fewer people and they live farther apart. Anyone who has seen the embattled citizens of small villages choosing up sides knows all about that. It is not because they are particularly cussed; rather, it is because people are made that way. In the city or suburbs you can be anonymous, invisible, a nonparticipant, but in small town life you can't hide. You have to stand up and be counted. In a big city you can ride for blocks or miles and never see anyone you know, but hereabouts you cannot go a mile without being waved at or spoken to—even if it might sometimes be just a cursory "Hi!"

Those who complain about the unfriendliness of neighbors labor under the handicap of wanting to go too far too fast. I count myself a reasonably friendly fellow, but it takes me rather a long time to decide to become intimate. If I discover that the pleasant person I met for the first time a couple of weeks ago is showing up without warning every few days to have a cozy chat about nothing in particular, I'm apt to feel as scared as Robinson Crusoe was when he discovered a footprint in the sand—evidence that he no longer had his privacy.

The business of nonacceptance resides principally in the mind of the person who feels rejected, not in the action of any particular group of people. In all societies there are some who love nothing better than to "rap," and the subject of their conversation is unimportant. What is paramount is that they feel warmed by the companionship of a group of similar-minded folk. There are others, not unfriendly or antagonistic, who have so much going on in their own minds that they never feel lonely or in need of society. The psychiatrists label this group as less well adjusted, less able to be cooperators in the business of living, but I disagree; I think this is just another theory to fill a hole in an idea social scientists have decided on *a priori*.

Of course I know that my own predilections are colored by my inheritance, just as are those of others. A solitary childhood under the care of Victorian grandparents is about as far removed from growing up in the crowded world of today as one can imagine. There is also the fact that I never even spoke on a telephone until I was about eighteen years of age, whereas my grandchildren have their own phones by their beds. I think this is why I dislike conversing on a telephone. When I make a call I do so for a specific reason, and when I answer the phone I expect to be asked a question I can answer and then hang up. I find it difficult merely to chitchat.

The telephone is an enormously useful invention but a pestiferous nuisance. When I was in business I used to say that, if I were not careful, people I would not let into my office in person would waste my time on the telephone instead. Most people alive now either never knew or have forgotten that many cities used to have more than one telephone system and one was for business calls only. In Philadelphia the second company had a slogan: "When the Keystone rings, it is a business call."

If you enjoy small talk you will surely find companions everywhere. There are plenty of people in Maine who fit into this category—people who will happily sit over a cup of coffee and chat at any odd time. However, there are also here, and everywhere, those who prefer their own company but whom it would be quite wrong to stigmatize as unfriendly. This is something you must accept if you want to live in the country.

Rubbish and Trumpery

When I was a boy, there was a saying among the grown-up members of my family that if you kept anything for seven years you would find a use for it. (When I say my family, I include not only those related by blood or marriage but also the larger family that included all the residents of our village.) The adage was, in fact, one of universal belief, an axiom of rural society.

Nowadays articles are made with the express intent that they be discarded as soon as they show signs of wear, or perhaps when there is no wear at all, as in the case of bottles that may have outlived their original purpose. Things are even made to wear out in, say, seven years, thus relieving us of any decision making at all.

If one searches for the origin of this change of life style, it is apparent that when people live in close quarters they do not have space to keep things for seven years, and, if they change their place of habitation frequently, they prefer not to lug along a lot of miscellanea every time they move. The usual apartment is dimensioned to the inch. There are no cellars and no attics in which to lodge useful (and useless) discards for the profit and delectation of future generations. I am reminded of Thoreau's description of one such collection:

January 27th 1854 — Attended the auction of Deacon Brown's effects a little while today—a great proportion of old traps, rubbish, or trumpery, which began to accumulate in his father's day and now, after lying half a century in his garret and other dustholes is not burned, but surviving neighbors collect and view it, and buy it, and carefully transport it to their garrets and dust holes, to lie there until their estates are settled, when it will start again. Among his effects was a dried tape-worm and various articles too numerous and worthless to mention. A pair of old snowshoes is almost regularly sold on these occasions, though none of this generation has seen them worn here.

When we bought Amen Farm we did not find much rubbish, certainly nothing of value, nor any tapeworms or snowshoes. Old Roy Bowden was notable as a "close" man. Before he sold the farm he had sold everything else he could talk anybody into paying for and had found some use for almost all he couldn't sell. One item he was unable to dispose of was a black horsehide coat. It had once been worn by Jack, the horse that pulled his delivery wagon. When, in the fullness of time, Jack passed into the great beyond, Roy had him skinned and made himself a coat from the tanned hide. Under urging from Roy, I once tried it on and found that it covered me like a Kurdish tent and weighed about as much. I was puzzled about how he was able to get around in it, as Roy was smaller than I. After a bit he confessed that he wore it only when he was sitting in his delivery wagon, so in a way Jack continued to make his appointed rounds even after his demise.

But like Shakespeare's Autolycus in *The Winter's Tale,* I have always been a snapper-up of unconsidered trifles. I suspect that the next owner of this place will have more fun than I did searching the "garret." All I ever discovered were a few horse liniment bottles and a couple of empty tins labeled "Bag Balm." I have now accumulated enough of my own old traps, rubbish, and trumpery for a diligent searcher to find almost anything. I am due for a yard sale.

I have been a nail straightener all my life and by now have saved enough to build a house, although I have no intention of doing so. Also, although I own enough woodlot to keep me warm until the devil takes over, I still save all sizable prunings and odd bits of board that come my way. There was a day when wooden boxes were in general use as shipping containers, but that time is long past—most things, even French wines, are now shipped in cardboard cartons—so I can no longer add boxes to my kindling, but when any really large cartons appear on the scene, I recycle them into brooders for my annual batch of chicks. I could, of course, buy a brooder, but to an old-fashioned recycler the idea of paying for something that can be made out of someone else's discards is anathema.

I think that most people enjoy collecting junk, although there are some like my mother-in-law, who used to keep extraneous material at a minimum. She did not like old junk and would have, I think, thrown out all her antique furniture and substituted stainless steel as being more sanitary if she had had any idea that we would have helped her. But, as I say, I am not of that genre; I snap up trifles whenever and wherever I find them.

As I sit in my study all I have to do is to cast my eyes around to confirm my proclivity. On my desk is a very cheap glass paperweight in which (though so indistinct as to be almost invisible) can be seen the words "State of Maine." It serves no useful purpose as I have several other paperweights that are much more attractive. "State of Maine" refuses to maintain its balance unless it is on a perfectly level surface, which a pile of papers (my pile anyway) never is, but I could no more throw it away than I could discard the thirty-five-year-old jacket that I wear in the garden. In the lap drawer of the desk on which the paperweight lives are eight assorted pens, most of the ballpoint type, only one of which works. I know I should have thrown them out long ago, but they look so new and gay in their red and green and blue and silver coloring that I cannot bring myself to do it. I am sure I will find a use for them, although, to be honest, I see no useful resurrection for a bloodless plastic pen.

Although I have not smoked a cigar for a decade, one has been in my desk for as long as I can remember. It must have been given to me at a christening. It is a La Corona, which I believe is the imprimatur of royalty amongst cigars, and if I were offered another tomorrow, I would snap it up with alacrity. Nearby are two small packages, resembling rolls of dimes, that are labeled Haw Flakes, followed by an inscription in Japanese, which is not one of my languages. I opened one and found that it contained tissue-thin disks of a strange-tasting substance that I suppose is an Oriental version of the old Sen-Sen tablets I used to suck as a boy under the erroneous impression that they would deceive people into thinking I had not been smoking. I am waiting for some child to appear to whom I can give these.

On the bookshelf behind me are several circular plastic margarine containers that will be perfect for seeds if I ever remember to save any. Beside them is a piece of flint from the wall surrounding the school I attended seventy-odd years ago. I pried it out of the wall the last time I was there (it was loose—I mention this to minimize my vandalism) and carried it all the way across the Atlantic. While on the subject of rocks, I should take the opportunity to remind you to avoid stumbling over an oval granite stone I brought home one day from Marshall's Island. I had the idea of using it as a doorstop, but as the door by which it lies is never opened for more than long enough to permit entry, it merely serves to trip people.

On the mantel over the fireplace is a small square of pasteboard with an even smaller bit of paper mounted on it that once was a sepia sketch of a Friendship Sloop. *I* know what it is because the vessel's outline is photographically impressed on the retina of my memory, but everyone else wonders what on earth that little blank piece of paper is doing on my mantel. Next to it is a bronze relief of Napoleon, Empereur. His presence makes a bit more sense, because years ago one of my ancestors was his jailor on the island of St. Helena, but since I was brought up to think of Napoleon as we now regard Hitler, it does *not* make much sense to have his likeness where I have to see it every day. Stuck partly behind Napoleon is a cartoon of myself shaking unwanted calls out of a telephone into a wastebasket. It was sent me by the cartoonist after I had written a column about how much I hate answering the telephone.

I have, of course, innumerable cases containing superannuated spectacles. As I have been wearing glasses for a matter of forty years and had to change them frequently when younger, I have quite a collection. I think I shall have to instruct my lawyer to prepare a codicil to my will leaving them to the Salvation Army, for I know I shall continue to treasure them jealously for as long as I live.

Then, in the medicine cabinet, there are several small china dishes bought because they were so "cute." They contain such treasures as a gold filling that popped out one day when I was cracking Brazil nuts with my teeth (a practice I have since avoided), some Mexaforma tablets I used to carry when I traveled in Latin America (they were intended to defeat Montezuma's curse, but since I have not been there in a decade their future utility is doubtful), and a small tin that once contained boracic acid ointment. The tin's top is ornamented with the initials B-P, meaning I know not what, and the name and address of the maker: Smawson & Sons Ltd, Barnet, England. I cannot recall ever visiting Barnet, but every time I pick up the tin to throw it away I am struck by the niceness of the fit of the lid—so accurate that the tin must have some future usefulness—and I put it back in the cabinet.

I don't see any modern Shakespeare on the horizon to immortalize my habits as was done for Autolycus, but the executors who will be burdened with the job of disposing of all this junk after I die will remember me for one lifetime anyway, and treasure hunters at the auction will enjoy a goodly portion of rubbish and trumpery.

A Master of His Craft

I have a desk in my little garden house that I especially cherish because it was made for me by a friend. He is an old cabinet maker who is worthy of the designation "craftsman," and everything he constructs gives evidence of that fact. A notable appraiser of valuable furniture who was visiting me recently ran his hand over it, knelt to observe the perfect fit of the drawers and the care that had been taken to be sure the grain of the paneling matched, and said, "Now, that desk was made by a master of his craft."

The top of the desk is made from the drop-leaf of a Victorian table. I never saw the table entire, but it was obviously no ordinary piece of furniture. The part I have consists of two one-inch-thick, straight-grained, perfectly clear oak boards, one of them fourteen inches wide and the other only slightly less, that are as level and smooth over their whole surface as a millpond in the calm of early morning. The top has a decorative edge of deeply incised carving.

The desk has added significance for me because, except for the top, it is made of wood from an ancient barn that once stood on my farm in Pennsylvania. The house I lived in there was very old indeed, but the barn was more recent, though sufficiently venerable to have been constructed in the days when American chestnut trees were common enough to be used for building timber, for that is what the barn was made of. Certainly more than a century and a half of storms and sunshine had passed over it. Through hard use and neglect the barn had fallen upon evil times, and when it came into my hands the roof showed gaping holes and the massive timbers underpinning its floor had rotted at the ends and fallen into the tie-up. Despite these disasters, there was enough sound lumber left to enable me to make the old house habitable again and provide additional materials for other ventures.

I never sit at the desk without wondering about my predecessors in ownership, both of the table and of the barn. Objects honestly and pridefully made for man's use acquire over the years a personality of their own; they gain character. This is why people buy "antiques" and set high value on things owned and used by past generations. Today's mass-produced, machine-made artifacts are soulless, no matter how expensive or convenient they may be. What they lack is the touch of a craftsman who is deeply interested in both what he is making and the needs of the person for whom it is being made. It may be a house, a desk, or even just a small tool such as I use in the spring to cut asparagus. It is not the size or value or importance of the thing being made, but the honesty and skill with which the work is done.

I don't know who made my asparagus knife, nor if it was made for that purpose, but its curved steel blade was obviously hammered out and tempered by a local blacksmith who was keenly interested in what he was doing. Even its small, pear-shaped wooden handle—turned, no doubt, on a village lathe—was made by a man who found the time to incise a thin decorative line around its largest circumference. I suspect that the knife may have been used originally by a cobbler to cut leather, as I dimly recollect having seen such a tool in the hands of a harness maker in my youth.

I am fortunate that my own employment, for a large part of my life, and my avocations at other times, have been interesting and rewarding. Not rewarding in money alone, because economic rewards, though necessary, are barren of themselves and leave a man's soul unfulfilled unless there is something in his work that is satisfying, something that he would want to do even if there were no spur of necessity. I am sure that much of today's restlessness is directly attributable to this deprivation. Economically, almost all working people are better off now than they were in the past, but we all need more than money to satisfy our deepest yearnings.

The man who made my desk put himself into it. It was his creation, and he was happy and proud of his work. He was glad that I would use it in my own creative employment, knowing that I too would do my best and that the desk would continue to be useful and give pleasure to still other generations when we both are dead.

Grapefruit and a Bouillon Cube

I am an expert on how easy it is to shed weight. Like the man who argued that it was easy to give up smoking—he had done it hundreds of times—I have reduced my poundage at least that frequently. The difficulty is that, somehow, after I have taken to drinking preprandial martinis again, I see with astonishment when I step on the scale after my morning shower that I am five pounds heavier than I was before. I shrug it off as an aberration due to the fact that I went to too many parties the previous week, and now that I have nothing to do but stay at home and work, my weight will soon be back to normal. Of course, I have a bit of trouble determining what is normal; however, I have a number of diet books I can consult. One has a snapshot of me stapled onto the back cover. The picture is old now, having been taken ten years ago, but it still scares me. My wife snapped it when I was not looking and got a profile that pictures me leaning backward to keep my balance, like a pregnant woman.

In years past, some people were fat and some were thin, just as is the case today, but nobody ever thought anything needed to be done about it. They just figured it as a visitation from the Lord, like brown eyes or curly hair or short stature. If Uncle Joe was obese (stout, they called it) or if Aunt Lizzie was like a rail, they said it ran in the family. Nobody ever got exercised about it. Diets were unknown, except that beef tea and calfsfoot jelly were given to invalids (what, by the way, has happened to invalids?), and in Ireland women in that "interesting condition" were urged to drink stout. I guess that was what made the fortune of the Guinness Brewery. It was not until later that diabetics were warned against sugar, and much later still that people with heart problems were told not to eat fats. The notion that there is something reprehensible about being overweight, something slightly immoral, is a recent view. I have a notion that it came in with women's magazines that are full of "easy" diets, although how that surmise stacks up against the fact that those magazines get a large part of their advertising from food manufacturers I admit I can't explain.

Personally, I think it would have been wonderful to have lived in the eighteenth century. The meals our ancestors put away were unbelievable. I am sorry that I am not old enough to have experienced them, but I am able to read about them (and do), and furthermore, some remnants of the notion that a lot of food is not harmful lingered on into my childhood in the Edwardian period. I speak, of course, of the people who had money enough to afford gargantuan meals, not the millions who had (and still have) flat wallets and flat bellies.

If anyone had then suggested to those good Edwardians that the day be built upon a foundation of orange juice and Wheaties, he would have risked being committed. Most breakfasts in my youth did not even offer orange juice or grapefruit. Some hardy souls drank beer, but the suggestion that one should start the day by assaulting one's stomach with acidulous fruit juice would have been greeted with ribald laughter. Breakfast did include hot oatmeal, if you had to have cereal, as well as eggs, ham, bacon, fish cakes, hotcakes and maple syrup, toast, sausages, scrapple, almost anything else that was in season, and, of course, always pie. There was always a large pot of real coffee on the stove, not ersatz instant stuff, and lots of honest-to-God cream that came from a cow, her milk having been allowed to sit all night for the cream to rise to the top. The English sideboards of my youth, from which breakfasters helped themselves (a custom that still survives in country houses), were loaded with additional goodies that included kippers and bloaters, broiled kidneys and bacon, mutton chops, partridges, and a smoked haddock that you decorated with a couple of poached eggs and a ladleful of Hollandaise sauce. Since the egg has fallen into such disfavor with the cardiovascular crowd, it is not improper to mention that fried eggs were served, in both England and America, by the dozen on large white ironstone platters that occupied the place of honor in the middle of things.

If the fairies were to give me one wish, it would be that my metabolism be rearranged so that it resembles that of a few people I know. There is one man (whose name I won't mention, but everyone around here knows him) who, at past ninety (well past) still does a day's work as an electrician and can eat anything he chooses and never gain a pound. He is tall and thin and can climb a ladder as well now as when he was a boy. Food has not hurt him a bit. In the days when we had an old-fashioned Town Meeting and the ladies served a lunch between halves, he would polish off everything that was put on his plate (which was plenty, because his appetite was well known) and then ask how many kinds of pie were being served. If there were four—and there were usually at least that many—he would eat one piece of each. He said he didn't want to slight anybody.

Every time I open a household magazine I find a new "diet" being peddled. There was, and probably still is, the Mayo Clinic Diet (nothing to do with the Mayo Clinic) that starved you on grapefruit, spinach, and eggs; there were the Canadian Mounted Police Diet, the all-liquid diet, the no bread or pastry diet; and now we have the Scarsdale Diet. I have tried 'em all and am now working on the Scarsdale version. You are not supposed to stay on it for more than two weeks. They tell you that it lacks certain essential elements of a satisfactory diet if it is maintained longer than that. They need not worry; I have been a practicing Scarsdaler for days, and every time I pass the refrigerator I open the door to prove to myself that my resolve is ironclad. If I make it for three more, that will be Sunday, the day I never fail to have a glass of sherry and a *petit beurre* when I get home from church. I can already smell the aromatic fumes of the sherry and see the little drops sliding down the glass. If you think I am going to eat half a grapfruit and a bouillon cube dissolved in hot water, you credit me with a resolution I lack.

A Sword and Buckler

I have often thought that if it were not for books we would all be savages. We are all born savages; if you doubt it, read Robert Audrey's *African Genesis*. It is only through the accumulated experience of the ages that we grow into civilized beings. Not too civilized at that.

Without books we would know next to nothing of the past and be able to convey little to the future. Our scientists would be unable to build upon the discoveries and avoid the mistakes of their predecessors. There would be no Bible, no Shakespeare, no Cervantes, and no Goethe—no Alice in Wonderland, and no Edna St. Vincent Millay.

Our moderns say, "You could put it on tape," but the truth is that we are more eye-minded than ear-minded. Then, too, we would lose the beauty of our language, for few people talk as they write.

Books are our sword and buckler, the weapons of civilization. They have survived cataclysms, guarded and hidden and treasured to keep alive man's hopes for a better world.

One does not give it much thought, but throughout New England—and, I should suppose, most of the country—the small libraries, and many of the large ones, are there because they were privately built and endowed. It was and is the private citizen who creates and supports libraries. Andrew Carnegie alone built more than twenty-five hundred. The great libraries of the world are the repositories of knowledge beyond all conception, but it is the small library that feeds and fashions the mind of youth.

One of my earliest recollections is of a library. There were books in my grandparents' home where I lived, of course, but a nearby public library, housed in a two-storied building, with stacks on the ground floor and reading room above, stays best in my memory.

The librarian was hidden behind a glass divider that extended from counter level to the ceiling. Through it could be observed rows of numbers interspersed with blanks. To obtain a book, you consulted an index to find its number. If that number appeared behind the glass, the book was available; if there was a blank, it was not. The librarian came to a little hutch in the wall when you banged a bell and gave you the books of your choice, stamped your library card, and marked its number on a slip that she then inserted in the holder, turned end-for-end so that it now showed blank.

All of this was very inefficient, I'm sure, but in those leisurely days time played second fiddle to humanity. The librarian always had time to talk to small boys and make suggestions. I am sure that I had no idea my reading was being directed, but it was, and guided well. I read Henty, Ballantyne, and Marryat, and Dana, and Cooper, and any other book that seemed from its title to hold possibilities of adventure. I was greatly attracted by Jerome K. Jerome's *Three Men in a Boat*; the title sounded wonderful, but as far as I was concerned, it was a deception. It was not until I was grown that I chuckled over the misadventures of the trio during their trip up the Thames.

The smallest libraries that ever blessed me were the boxes of books suppied by the Merchant Marine Library Association. *Walden* came to me via the MMLA box, and I read it while lying on a top bunk in the fo'c'sle of a ship called the *Black Arrow* while the rats ran a tightrope along the steam pipes over my head. The rats chewed the back off a copy of White's *Selborne,* but I guess Thoreau was too tough for them.

Many things enter into the making of a man. When I look back over those long years at sea, and the longer years since, I have no doubt that the most powerful and beneficial influence of any has been the books that have been my constant companions.

I have my own share of books, some 5000 at last count. They are my friends and frequently bring me comfort, but I must admit that my wife, who looks upon my squirreling with more charity than any husband could reasonably expect, finally broke down and said, "I can't for the life of me understand why you want to buy *The Endemic Flora of Tasmania.*" The only valid reason I could advance was that I already owned volume one and that it would be silly not to get the remaining seven as they are published.

I feel a bit that way about magazines too. One corner of my attic is reserved as a storage area for periodical literature. With few exceptions, the stacks of magazines piled there do not date from before 1958 because that is when we moved to this house. As I never expect to leave here except on my final journey (when I do not anticipate being able to take anything with me) the stacks will undoubtedly grow taller until the terminal date arrives. Helen has suggested periodically that at least some of the magazines ("You never look at them!") be discarded before the weight of the pile cracks the kitchen ceiling. I don't disagree with her; I have long since learned that the passport to a tranquil marital life is to not dispute the wishes of the distaff side of the partnership. Of coure, not disagreeing does not necessarily commit one to agreement.

What usually happens is that, being pressed, I dutifully proceed up to the attic to survey the task that lies before me and decide how to go about it, for no wise man embarks upon a major undertaking without a plan.

If it is winter, I soon find it too cold to work until warmer weather. Summer in coastal Maine seldom gets too hot, so I can't use that argument. What I do (and this is without forethought—it just comes upon me) is to begin to sort over the various piles to be sure that I do not extract randomly half a dozen issues from half a dozen different years. If my collection is to be reduced, it should be done methodically, and an entire file (say, of 1958) removed intact. This is where delay sets in. While the varrious journals were selectively piled, inevitably over the passage of a decade or so they got out of order, and I discover that one month of *Yankee* for 1958 has been mysteriously substituted for one from 1963. This involves my sitting on the floor and reassembling the numbers by year. *Yankee,* being a pocket-sized magazine, is extremely difficult to pile without the stack assuming the aspect of the leaning tower of Pisa and then, when my back is turned, falling and sliding into the onions with which they share floor space.

About this time I realize that the only way I can handle the situation is by tying each year in a separate bundle, so I groan to my feet and hobble downstairs for some string. As I go by Helen's office/sewing room, she asks encouragingly, "How are you doing?" I reply in the labored tones of a man engaged in an arduous task, "Pretty well, pretty well. I have to get some string."

Half an hour later I get back with some string, having taken time out for coffee, and at once run across an issue with an advertisement for a farm with a ten-room house, two barns, a fenced paddock, a trout pond, a stream, and three hundred acres of virgin mountainside in the Northeast Kingdom for sale for $11,000. I say to Helen, forgetting in my excitement that she is downstairs, "Hey, look at this! You can still buy a place cheap in Vermont." Then I turn the cover and find that I'm looking at an issue from April 1943 that somehow got carried over from my previous abode.

The only magazine for which I still have every issue is *Country Life,* an English weekly that countrymen of any nationality become addicted to after reading their first copy. My collection goes back to those austere days after the Second World War when Britons had even less to eat than during the war; through 1953, when all London burst into an extravaganza of bunting and window boxes to celebrate the coronation of Elizabeth II; then on and on, up hill and down dale, to her twenty-fifth anniversary in 1978, and beyond. They provide a written and pictorial history of a nation's countryside for a span of more than thirty years. How can I throw them out, even if I never reread them?

National Geographics are, of course, indestructible. They are so tightly bound that they won't burn. They won't sink if you throw them in the ocean, and nowadays you can't even give them to your local school or dentist. No one throws them out—the minute you open a copy you are transported to the jungles of Brazil, or fascinated by a picture of our astronauts disporting themselves on the moon. The only way to kick the habit is to walk away from them at the end of the subscription and leave the piles in the attic of a house you've sold to someone else.

The magazines in our attic range from the *American Scholar* and *Harvard* magazine to ephemera like book catalogues and garden seed lists. About the only publications nonresident are women's magazines—not that we don't buy them, but that is my wife's department, and she is stronger willed than I and gets rid of them promptly. She doesn't destroy them, but out of her kindness gives them to others, who, unable to refuse her generosity, take them home and store them in *their* attics.

The Garden and the Land

*God Almighty first planned a garden; and indeed it is
the purest of human pleasures.*

— Francis Bacon, *Essays*, XLVI, 1625

If a man owns land, the land owns him.

— R.W. Emerson, *Wealth*, 1860

Fa'min'

When I came here, I expected to farm this place. Not in a big way, of course; it only amounts to about eighty acres, and most of that is woods, but I had grown and harvested fine bright crops of oats on fields as small as two acres where I came from. My fields here are bigger, and I know that oats grow well, so after spending three years building up the land, I planted eight acres and got a clean crop. So far, so good, but then came the rub: I couldn't get them harvested. There was not a combine within a hundred miles, so I had to cut the oats for hay. An old neighbor remarked, "That's mighty fine hay. Got a lot of grain in it." That was when I bought a couple of Guernsey cows.

I hear a lot of conversation about home farms on the coast of Maine, but to operate one that carries more than a vegetable garden and a few animals is difficult, if not impossible. Small-time farmers can't afford to own all their equipment, so farming must be a cooperative venture. Nobody can own a combine and let it sit in the shed all but a few days of the year. Most can't even afford a baler, and hay is all baled nowadays. Bucolic visions of happy girls and boys pitching hay up into the mow belong on Currier and Ives prints.

I have more equipment than most. Besides a good powerful (for its day) tractor, I have a two-bottom plow, a side-delivery rake, a lime and fertilizer spreader, a seeder, a front-end loader, a disc harrow, and a Scotch harrow. The latter is used for smoothing out seedbeds and breaking up cow flops in pastures. I have a circular saw that operates off the tractor's power take-off and several skids for getting logs out of the woods. I don't own either a combine or a baler and do not have access to the first. It would cost too much to hire the only baler around.

People have a notion that with a little ingenuity and hard work anybody can take some run-down land and make a Malabar Farm out of it. It sounds good, but I would like to have had a look at Louis Bromfield's expenses. I employed a gardener once who had worked on Malabar Farm. He was a crackerjack gardener. He had been to Kew Gardens and was a graduate of Wisley in England. He knew a lot more about gardening than I did (which I have found unusual in America, where a gardener is commonly thought of as just a lawn cutter and weed puller). Anyway, he told me some of the things they did at Malabar and how many men they had working there. Indeed, a lot of wisdom, planning, and experience were put into the place, but there was also a lot of money.

I'll give you an idea of what it takes to "Malabarize" a run-down farm—not even a whole farm, just a bit of it. I can't give you the dollar amount because I gave up keeping track—it was too discouraging. When I came here the barn, like most old barns, looked like a swaybacked horse. I knew what I was getting into—I had seen barns before—but you can no more run a farm without a barn than you can operate a restaurant without a kitchen, so I propped up its backbone. While doing so, I discovered that my barn was really two barns placed end-to-end. Mainers are fond of moving buildings around, and when some farmer in the distant past wanted a bigger barn here he just moved one across the snow one winter.

My guest house (a store when I bought it) was moved here from the village about sixty years ago. It had been a paperhanger's shop for fifty years before that. Old Roy Bowden had a picture of it being hauled the three miles from the village behind half a dozen teams of oxen. Anyway, by the time I had put in a new ridgepole and jacked up the corners and replaced the rotten sills and cemented back the stone cornerposts, it was possible to walk across the floor without worrying that the place would collapse around your ears.

When I totted up the square footage, I discovered that if I put all my equipment in the barn there would not be room for anything else. No room for chickens or cows or sheep or any other livestock. Consequently, what could I do but build an extension all along one side for a henhouse and implement shed?

There were other items like water and light, and enough heat in the milk room to keep things from freezing, but I'll not discourage you further.

Having done these things and spent ten or fifteen thousand 1960 dollars, I went to work on the fields. For three years before I could get even a wisp of hay off them, I plowed, harrowed, limed, fertilized, planted, cut, and turned under three crops of green fertilizer a year—one of winter rye and two of Japanese millet. Nonfarmers have an idea that you can cut whatever grows up in an old field and it is hay. It is not. It is weeds, and if your cows have no better sense, or are starving to death, they may eat it, but it won't do them any good. They will just starve more slowly. About once a year someone asks me if I wouldn't like to mow his fields in return for the "hay"—and probably thinks I am not very neighborly when I decline.

My pasture and hayfield are better than most around here, but

THE GARDEN AND THE LAND

before I plowed under the nine consecutive green crops, the hay field was a wilderness of wild roses, blueberries, Indian paintbrush, and half a dozen other perennial weeds, enlivened with odd clumps of puckerbrush, bayberry, and alder and studded with a goodly number of sheep-sized boulders. At almost any time of year it was an artist's delight, but no place to provide the wherewithal to feed either man or beast, except deer and fieldmice. I found later that the deer are pretty smart, too, because they appeared in much greater numbers after I had some civilized crops growing. The one thing I did have going for me was that the soil was sandy loam. It was as poor as Job's turkey, and even after I had my cover crops turned under, any fertilizer spread on it went straight to China (China, China—not China, Maine). It could have been worse; much of the land in coastal Maine is marine clay, which takes so long to warm up in the spring that you can't get a crop off it before autumn frost.

However, I persevered for about five years and lost a little less money each season. I tried to run it as a business, and the gentlemen from the Iternal Revenue Service were understanding, but affairs got to the point where I knew, and I knew they knew I knew, that I was never going to make a profit, so I reluctantly closed my books on the venture. Since then I have kept a few animals to put in my own freezer and raised enough chickens and collected enough eggs to supply ourselves and a few friends—and I've taken great care not to ask my wife (who is an accountant) how much we are in the hole.

If you are young and can do all your own work (which I can't), and you don't get too expansive, you can probably operate what the English call a smallholding. You can raise vegetables, of course; even the smallest plot of ground, so long as it is not hedged in by sky-scrapers or completely shaded by trees, can be made to produce vegetables. You don't even need experience. If you can read (and I admit many people can't) and are sufficiently competent mentally to follow instructions, you can buy or borrow *Crockett's Victory Garden,* do what he says, and—presto—you are in business.

The English smallholder usually grows a cash crop in addition to feeding his family. Feeding the family might include keeping a few rabbits, perhaps even a lamb or a steer, but there is no attempt to go beyond what can be done by one man aided by his wife and children. The cash crop in England might consist of strawberries or black currants, some other soft fruit, or perhaps asparagus and rhubarb. In

Maine, it could well be cultivated blueberries, but you must not get too big, for as soon as you have to employ help you are in trouble.

Young back-to-the-landers frequently come to see me, and I do my best to steer them away from large animals. In the first place, few people have had any experience handling cattle, or even sheep, and it never occurs to them that their handsome, healthy cow could show up one morning with the feet of a dead calf sticking out of her vulva and that they will have to do a little obstetrical job while sliding around on cowflops in the middle of a stony field. Fortunately, most are content to work with goats (good for both meat and milk) and perhaps a pig. Nowadays, unless you are located in a district where there are enough large animals to make it possible for a veterinarian to make a living working with them, you will discover that your local vet only looks after cats and dogs and parakeets, and won't come out to look after anything bigger.

I gave up keeping cattle for a number of reasons. One was that I had to keep a bull and the other was that I found I was a little too old to be chasing a bull. Not very many years ago I could call a man in Bucksport when one of my cows came into season, and he could be here in a flash with his little black bag. He was the artificial inseminator for the area and he could provide a choice of semen from any number of bulls of different breeds. The cow was not consulted and seemed sort of bored with the whole deal, but it worked. It saved the farmer (me) from the expense of feeding and keeping a bull behind a fence all year. The service fee was nominal—three or four dollars, if I recall correctly, and if it didn't take, the next one was on the house. There are no longer enough cows around to keep the inseminator in business. Twenty-five years ago there must have been a score of family cows in our village alone, and fifty years gone it was the rare family that did *not* have a cow tethered somewhere nearby and a pig in the back yard.

It is not my intention to be discouraging, but merely to warn people who should not be in the country anyway. Country life, farming and all that, is not for everyone. It certainly is not something to run to when the going gets tough in the city. If you are young and have a little money and are willing to work hard for long hours with no union contract or tenure to fall back on—come ahead. If you really are "country" no matter where you come from, your rewards will so far outweigh the sacrifices that you will consider yourself a resident of the best of all worlds.

THE GARDEN AND THE LAND

A Plenitude of Boulders

Amen Farm, like most country places in Maine, or in New England generally for that matter, is blessed with a plenitude of boulders. They range from little ones the size of a bushel basket to monsters whose backs only slightly emerge from the ground, looking like the barnacle-encrusted shells of enormous turtles awash in a tropical ocean. There were a number of the latter dimension in what is now our hayfield when we came here. The field was a wilderness of Indian paintbrush, witchgrass, wild blueberries, roses, bayberry, and every other variety of vegetation that will grow without the intervention of the hand of man. It was an artist's delight, and mine too, for that matter, except that it satisfied only the eye, whereas I wanted the land to produce a useful crop that would in a small way contribute to my living.

I pondered for some time about what I should do to that field. The soil was thin, hungry, sandy loam over gravel, and I knew I had to get some compost into it. Making compost for a vegetable plot by mulching it with hay as is recommended by the redoubtable Mrs. Stout is one thing, but building up ten acres of barren field is another. I had the soil tested but already knew what it needed, which was just about everything, including ground limestone (which holds longer than processed lime) plus a balanced fertilizer, and continuous working to eliminate the woody growth and add humus. The first thing was to mow it so the plow could turn a reasonably clean furrow in the root-laden ground, and the second was to plant some cover crops to be turned over to enrich the soil.

It was when I first tried to plow the field that I discovered the sunken boulders. I owned what was for the time a reasonably powerful Oliver tractor and a two-bottom plow. (I still own them and they still perform well.) After struggling across the field a few times, I decided that though it would be a long job, I could, in time, accomplish it. I came in to tell my wife of my progress so she could praise me, and it was shortly after I went back to work that my pride was humbled: I ran headlong into a boulder about as big as a bull that was buried not more than two inches below the surface. There was a great deal of grinding and clashing of metal. The tractor stalled, and if I had not had a good grip on the wheel, I would have been pitched onto the ground. If you are a seafaring rather than a farming type, you know how it feels on those rare (I hope) occasions when you fetch up, all unaware, on a submerged object you swear is not on the chart.

I discovered before I finished plowing that there were eight or ten of these behemoths lurking underground, in addition to the run-of-the-mill smaller ones weighing only a few hundred pounds that could be lugged off in a stone boat. You may think that one boulder to the acre is nothing to complain about, but they are much more of a hazard in a field than is a half-tide rock in the ocean. The latter you are reminded of twice a day if you are around on the ebb tide, but there is no tide in my field except the green one that comes with the spring, and *that* just makes the ledge less visible.

I suppose that in the old days, when my predecessor, Roy Bowden, plowed the field with a horse and single-bottom plow that certainly did not dig very deeply, he merely eased the plow over the top of the boulder until it took hold again in deeper soil. From the look of the field, it had been a long time since Roy had done any plowing. He never struck me as one who was particularly attracted to vigorous exercise. About all he had done for many years in the way of farming was to cut the weeds (hay by courtesy) and gather them with an ancient spring-tooth rake to sell for blueberry hay.

I thought for a while of anchoring spar buoys on the boulders, as is done in the shoal water I can see from my piazza, but figured that I'd get a lot of inquiries from puzzled spectators, so I decided instead to blow up the rocks, as is done sometimes when there is a ledge in a ship channel. Having served in two wars and gotten in the way of a couple of swiftly moving objects, I early developed a deep and abiding respect for explosives. I am pretty cautious even when I use a 20-gauge shotgun to wing a partridge or a .22 to shoot rats, so I contracted with a gentleman from Blue Hill who is an explosives expert to do the job. He did all right, particularly on a boulder near the house. A flying splinter from that one did annihilate half of a small crabapple tree, but as it missed going through a window, all was well.

When the explosions had ceased, I surveyed the battlefield and discovered that there was still a lot of work to be done. I had thought in my innocence that the rocks, being shattered, could just be picked up and carried off. I was mistaken. The difficulty was that the explosive had merely split the boulders, so that if the bottom was five or ten feet deep before the blast, it was still in exactly the same place, only in smaller pieces afterwards. To get the rock out, I still had to dig a five- or ten-foot hole.

The fellows who farmed these rocky acres 150 years ago had the right idea: don't confront nature, just go around her. They had gunpowder too, and could have blown these boulders. They didn't try; they just accepted them as one of the unexplainable vicissitudes that the Lord, in his inscrutable wisdom, chose to visit on mankind—like Wescott's dictum that a reasonable number of fleas is good for a dog so as to keep him from broodin' over bein' a dog. What they did instead was to pile such other smaller boulders as they *could* lug off to the spot where the monster lay buried, thus, in time, making a cairn that bye the bye became covered with brush and maybe a wild apple tree, harboring the odd rabbit and sometimes a "pattridge" in the fall.

One of the things you have to learn if you live in the country is that you don't get much unsolicited advice. If you want to be a damn fool, your neighbors are likely to let you go ahead and enjoy yourself. In my case, knowing something of my country antecedents, they probably thought a few decades in the city had softened my brains and concluded that the best way to restore my sanity was by the rural version of the shock treatment given to patients in mental institutions. It worked!

Too Much Altitude

One of the troubles with being a grown-up, besides the obvious ones of having to go to work and pay taxes, is that you are too far from things. You have too much altitude. I was in the garden this afternoon, planting peppers (Park's Whopper, to be exact) when the heat got to me. I also had gravel in my shoes. My wife says I can get gravel in my shoes walking across the parlor rug, but be that as it may, I decided to lay me down for a few minutes under the shade of a Chinese chestnut tree—one that never rewards me with nuts but is pleasant to look upon. A fringe benefit of this decision was that I had to get down from my normal height (not something calling for a pressurized cabin, but too far away to be on a level with small things) to about a foot or so, which was where I spent a large part of my time grubbing around when young.

There is a saying that more grows in the garden than the gardener plants (which is also true of the mind), and one of the most omnipresent of these in my garden is devil's paintbrush. I think its yellow and orange blossoms, mixed with buttercups and daisies, are among the loveliest sights of our Maine fields, but I don't want them in mine. Even less do I want them in my lawn, where they are as difficult to eradicate as original sin. However, in my lowly position under the chestnut tree, I found some on a level with my eyes, and for the first time in a great many years I saw them as I did when a child. I plucked one and held it up to the blue sky. I observed it as through a microscope rather than a telescope, and all the magic of my boyhood flooded back. It had really never gone; it had just been waiting there patiently in the wings for me to give it a chance to emerge from the overlay of other things that I have thought, erroneously, to be more important in these latter years.

The thing that I noticed particularly about the flower was that the petals—there are rows of them surrounding what appears to be a central boss of stamens—appeared to have been trimmed with pinking shears. Each one had five teeth as regular as those on a fine saw, and down the back of the outer row of petals was a stripe of orange-red. Actually, there is no separate group of stamens, for each petal carries one clutched in its base and is capable of producing a seed, which is also true of dandelions and explains why they are such prolific seeders and so difficult to get rid of. Hawkweed, though, is a much more formidable enemy than the dandelion because, in addition to prolific seeding, it creeps along the ground, rooting every few inches, so it can, and will, take over an entire lawn if measures are not taken to stop it.

I suppose you expect me to tell what those measures are, but you are going to be disappointed because I do not know of any surefire cure. One of the most pleasant ones is to sit on the ground on a comfortably warm day and hook up one of the tentacles with a hand cultivator, follow it through to the parent plant, and ease out the whole business. This method will, naturally enough, work only if your lawn is small and you are blessed with patience and plenty of time. There are weed killers available, and I have tried a few without much success, probably becaue I did not apply them at the correct time or in sufficient amounts. I am scary about weed killers on my lawn. If you are treating a golf course, that is one thing, but my lawns are small and surrounded by hedges and flower beds, and weed killers do not always stay where you put them.

A friend saw me when I returned from my expedition into my boyhood and said, "Wherever did you get that hat?" Looking at the sweatband, I saw that I bought it in Stetson's hat shop in Philadelphia on July 14, 1955. The date is imprinted along with my initials. It is a straw hat of the kind then called a boater and is still sound but for a small hole in one side. It is a trifle sunburnt, but so is its owner. In years gone by, I could have taken it to a shoeshine parlor, where an ancillary service was the blocking and cleaning of hats. Alas, there no longer seem to be any shoeshine parlors and certainly no hat cleaners. In this disposable society nothing lasts long enough to be cleaned or repaired, and if anything did, no one would have it renovated because it would be out of style, and God forbid that one should be caught wearing last year's model. Anyway, so far as I can observe, not many people even wear hats nowadays. Certainly those few who do wear headgear do not have the date of purchase recorded inside.

I think I shall have my hat cremated with me when I die, after the fashion of Hindu ladies committing suttee on their husbands' funeral pyres. I shall thus cheat the antiques dealers and have something to shelter my grey hairs from the perpetual sunshine of eternity—and remind me of my earthly garden.

Kuplink! Kuplank! Kuplunk!

An acquaintance, Robert McClosky, who lives on one of our offshore islands, writes and illustrates the most charming of children's books. Among these is one called *Blueberries for Sal*. Our grandchildren grew up on Bob McClosky, and my wife has all his books in a pile in the corner of her "office," whence she dispenses them to visiting small fry to pore over while spreadeagled on the floor. If that assortment of kids could be said to have a favorite, I think it is probably *Blueberries for Sal*.

One of the reasons they have preferred it is that we had a blueberry patch out back. I use the past tense because I have neglected it of late and it is now growing up with little spruces, bayberry, and puckerbrush. Helen queried me about it the other day, and I promised to mow the patch and burn it to get it back into shape. She reminded me that we now have a generation of great-grandchildren coming along who, with their friends, will be reading *Blueberries for Sal* and wanting to get a can and make their blueberries go "kuplink! kuplank! kuplunk!" just as Sal's did.

In Maine, gathering wild blueberries is a childhood privilege the memory of which lingers for many years. When children are young they pick the individual berries, but as they grow older they scorn picking and start raking. Either way, they never forget it. Part of the charm, in addition to kneeling or bending over the warm fragrance of the clean earth, is the feeling that they are gathering in summer's bounty for nothing.

Blueberrying when you're a kid is fun, but if you rake commercially you need an iron back with a hinge in it. Even gathering a few quarts on the home territory, when you get older, is hard on those who have back trouble— and that is most of us.

While I was still able to bend with a fair degree of comfort, I decided to anticipate my old age and plant some blueberries that I would not have to bend to gather. Accordingly, I read up on highbush blueberry culture, prepared the ground, and, when the time was right, bought an assortment of varieties and planted them. It turned out to be one of my better decisions.

Growing highbush blueberries is not difficult, but I don't know of anyone doing it on a large scale in Maine. Here the wild berry is king. It does not have to be cultivated in the way the highbush blueberry does, although of course the fields (or barrens, as they are sometimes called) have to be burned over at intervals to prune the plants and keep the weeds down. They do have to be sprayed to control the blueberry maggot, but otherwise they are left wild. Most highbush blueberries in the markets come from Michigan or New Jersey. It was in the latter state, at Whitesbog, that the first attempts were made to grow them commercially.

In my experience, highbush blueberries grow very well in Maine. From my twenty-five bushes I pick more than a hundred quarts a year and I do little to them except prune and fertilize. The berries are large, from five-eighths to three-quarters of an inch in diameter, and have a slightly different flavor from the wild berry. People who don't grow their own complain that the large berry is not as sweet as the wild one. This is because they have probably never eaten a fully ripe one. Picked at the right moment, when they fall from the bush into the hand, they are just as sweet and much juicier.

Obviously it is not possible to rake highbush blueberries. The plants grow six feet tall and the fruit hangs in a cluster, like grapes. The berries have to be picked one by one as they ripen over a period of weeks, depending on the variety. Harvesting is a labor-intensive business and cannot be done roughly. It has no relationship to the harvesting of wild berries, where the entire crop is taken at one time and the rakers follow a pattern of white strings to be sure that they do not miss an area.

We began picking this year on August 20 and will continue until frost, usually in October but sometimes even into November. The first frosts do not trouble us, as the berries are well up off the ground. I have even picked them after a light snow, but once they have been frozen (either in the field or in the freezer) they are not much good to eat raw. On the other hand, we eat frozen berries cooked in pies or cobbler all winter, and they are my favorite dessert.

I said before that growing highbush blueberries was not difficult, and it is not, but there are a few simple rules to observe: they must be planted in acid soil, they must be heavily mulched (preferably with sawdust), and they must be protected from birds.

Most soil in New England is acid and can be made more so by the addition of ammonium sulfate and a sawdust mulch. The rotting sawdust will keep the soil acid, but it uses nitrogen in the process of decay, and that needs to be replaced. I use chicken droppings and sawdust because our hens run a manure factory on the side. If you don't have poultry, you can do the job with ordinary commercial fertilizer—a 5-10-5 formula is satisfactory.

Birds are a big problem. Our berries are grown inside a cage of one-inch-mesh hen wire, but even so a few birds aways break in and spoil a lot of berries. They just take one or two bites and then move on to another. The amount of fruit they can ruin is amazing. I used to think that the French were dreadful because they ate little songbirds, but if I could catch the birds that afflict my blueberries, I'd eat them with pleasure.

Fall is the time to prepare the ground so you can plant next spring. Dig a hole, or preferably a bed, eighteen inches to two feet deep. Mix the soil with about 50 percent peat moss (wet), old sawdust, woods duff, or any other organic matter. Having done this, go back to the house, stir up a drink, elevate your feet, and read catalogs and books about how to grow blueberries until planting time next spring.

Highbush blueberries are partially self-sterile, so in order to get a good crop, plant at least four bushes in as many varieties. Those I have are Coville, Herbert, Jersey, and Ivanhoe. They vary a bit in size, flavor, and sweetness. It is hard to say which I prefer. I think perhaps it is Ivanhoe. The fruit is a little tart if picked early but develops a wonderfully sweet flavor if allowed to ripen. Coville is the latest of the berries we grow, and the fruit hangs on the bush long after a few light frosts.

Having studied the catalogs all winter, you should order your plants early and get them planted as soon as you can get them into the ground. A late frost won't hurt them a bit. Dig a hole in that nice bed you prepared and set them at least ten feet apart, no matter how little they look to you. Before very long they will be over your head and shaking hands with each other. If you have only a few plants, you can cover them with any kind of netting after the fruit sets. The birds will peck through the netting, but you will still have a lot of berries left. If you have more than a half dozen bushes, it is best to build a cage about seven feet high and as large as necessary to surround the plants. This is all you have to do except pick the berries. I can pick a quart in fifteen minutes.

BLUEBERRY COBBLER

Put a quart of berries (for four people) in a stainless steel or enamel kettle. Add sugar to taste—half a cup, maybe—and bring to a boil. Add 2½ tablespoons tapioca and cook for a few minutes. Don't add water; the frozen berries have plenty and the fresh berries you can squash.

When cooked, stir in a little cinnamon and pour into an ovenproof bowl. (We use a Bennington dish we bought in an antique shop.)

Make some Bisquick according to the recipe on the box (but add a pinch of salt) and drop a tablespoon of it for each diner on top of the blueberry mixture. Bake in a 375-degree oven for about twenty minutes, or until the Bisquick is brown.

The Destroying Angel

The indecent amount of rain we sometimes experience in the spring isn't all that good for the garden, but one interesting side effect is a bumper crop of mushrooms—or toadstools, as you may choose to call them. All over the lawns and in the woods they spring up "like mushrooms," to last for a day or so and then to vanish.

If you have been observant you will have noticed that fungi take strange forms. One of my compatriots in the office cornered me and said, "Just the man I want to see. You know all about plants. I found the strangest thing the other day. It looked exactly like an egg coming through the ground, and the next time I looked at it, it had hatched and something the shape and size of my little finger, with a red end on it, had broken through the shell."

"Did it stink?" I asked him.

"Did it stink? Brother, I'll say it did," he replied.

"That, my boy, was a stink-horn, a fungus called *Phallus impudicus,* and even if you have forgotten your schoolboy Latin you can figure out the translation."

The appearance of some fungi is quite unpredictable. In all my gardening life I have only seen *Phallus impudicus* a dozen times, and never in the same place twice. It has been observed, however, for centuries. John Gerarde refers to it in the 1633 edition of his herbal. Gerarde did not think much of mushrooms anyway. He quotes Galen, the Greek, as saying, "they are all very cold and moist, and therefore approach unto a venomous and murthering facultie . . . and most of them do suffocate and strangle the eater."

There is no botanical significance to the names *mushroom* and *toadstool.* They are all fungi, though the layman usually thinks of a mushroom as edible and a toadstool as poisonous. Actually, not many fungi are poisonous, though most are inedible because they are either tough or unpleasant tasting. The poisonous ones vary in their effects; some do no more than cause a mild stomach upset, while others will, as my granddaughter used to say, "kill you dead."

Among the most fatal of the fungi are the amanitas. One that has probably been seen by everyone who has ever walked in the woods is the fly agaric, *Amanita muscari,* with its red cap dotted with rough white spots. It looks dangerous, and is, but is not as bad as its relative with the yellowish crown, *Amanita phalloides,* which bears the common name of death cap. A couple of the amanitas are said to be dubiously edible, but nobody in his right mind would take a chance. They are best left where they grow; they have no place in the kitchen. By their names shall ye know them: deadly amanita, destroying angel, panther fungus.

Fungi, like other plants, have their season. The amanitas are more likely to be found in the fall, while others—among them the choicest of all from the point of view of the gourmet, the morels—appear in the spring. However, fungi can be found during any month of the year, including the dead of winter, when the artist's fungus, *Ganoderma applanatum,* shows up like giant scallop shells on the trunks of dying birches.

Whenever mushrooms are mentioned, people inquire immediately about their edibility. They view them only as something to eat. Actually, although only a few species are amenable to cultivation, all are enormously interesting, and some are beautiful when thought of as wild flowers. There is also one fungus, neither edible nor poisonous, that has been used for years by fishermen. It ia a species called *Formes fomentarius* that dry-fly enthusiasts know as amadou and use to dry their flies. I have had a piece in my tackle-box for twenty years. It feels like a bit of old chamois.

There are only a few wild mushrooms that I feel sure enough of to gather without at least mild apprehension. These are the morels, the shaggy manes, and the puffballs. They are hard to mistake. When I first moved to where I now live, puffballs popped up by the dozens in the flower borders. When they showed up again the following year I thought I had it made, a never-ending supply of puffballs. The next year there were only a couple, and there has not been one since. The appearance of puffballs, like other fungi, is unpredictable. The finest one I ever discovered was on a golf course. My companion was about to swing at it with his club until I cried to him in anguish, "My God, man, don't do that!" It was about eight inches in diameter and in perfect condition, the skin kid-glove smooth and the inside creamy white. To my taste, puffballs should be sliced about half an inch thick and simmered for a few minutes in a pan that a steak has been cooked in.

I have never found morels in the East, though they are said to be around and are common in parts of the Midwest. I regret their absence, as they are the best of the wild mushrooms. My experience with shaggy caps began when I tore down an old barn and bulldozed all the trash and the remains of the old manure pile into the hole. Next year shaggy caps were there by the dozen. They have to be gathered at just the right time, which is not long after they emerge from the ground. If left to develop, they soon collapse into an inky mess. Truffles, a subterranean mushroom, the delight of the gourmet and the ruin of his bank account, come mostly from France. They are said to grow wild in America, but I have never heard of one here, let alone seen one. The mushrooms we buy in the supermarket are all species of meadow mushrooms. They are common enough in the fields but I do not gather them, as there are others, similar in appearance, that are inedible and I do not know the difference. Sadly, mushrooms, like some wines, do not travel, and since we are not all lucky enough to live near Kennett Square, Pennsylvania, where half of the mushrooms in the United States are grown, we have to either use canned ones or put up with ones that are over the hill.

The only use I know of for the latter is in soup. My own quick recipe for cream of mushrom soup, indistinguishable from one made from scratch in your own kitchen, is a can of Campbell's plus a couple of cups of raw mushrooms. If the mushrooms have opened up and look weary, it does not matter. Add the usual can of milk to the soup, dump in the mushrooms, and put the whole business in the blender. Run it just long enough to break up but not liquify the mushroms. Heat and serve. Don't cook, and the flavor of raw mushrooms will come through. A dab of sour cream on top is a plus.

Mushrooms may be prepared in dozens of other ways. If really fresh ones are available, they are wonderful in a green salad, but they must be crisp when you slice them. We add them to almost all wok dishes, and they are good in stews. The secret is to add them at the last minute so they do not cook long enough to get rubbery. When I think of my childhood, I recall with longing the sideboards in country houses, where, among other delicacies, there would be broiled lamb kidneys and mushroom caps in gravy kept hot in silver dishes with little spirit lamps flashing beneath them.

Old Trees

Recently I was asked to speak to a group of ladies in Belfast about old-fashioned roses and thought that having already written a speech, I could use the same subject for my weekly column. But the sight of Belfast after an absence of some years reminded me of elm trees and what their loss means to our old New England towns.

The house where I was given lunch was not very old, but old enough to have once been covered by the elms that must have towered over it. It was built around 1835, and although I did not count the rings on the enormous butt that still remained in front of the house, its girth alone suggested that it was probably planted by the builder of the house. Exactly when does not matter, the point is that 150 years ago this street in Belfast was like innumerable other streets in innumerable other New England towns. The houses were new and the raw red of the bricks had not yet mellowed. The road, although paved, was not blacktopped, and the grass plots around the houses were deliberately kept small, for the lawnmower was a new invention and most people kept their grass neat with a sickle. There were vegetable gardens, and a few shrubs and flowers in each dooryard. There was plenty of manure for the gardens, for all the carriage houses sheltered a horse or two along with some variety of conveyance. Out front, between each house and the road, was a sapling elm tree. There were larger ones in front of older houses and a few that had seeded and grown without attention here and there in backyards, but generally the trees along the street were all elms of about the same age.

Although the scene is imaginary, it does suggest that the stately old elms would have started dying off in the fairly near future anyway, even without the advent of Dutch elm disease. While elms do live for a long time, they are no more immortal than we are, and had they lived out their natural lives, they would (just by the arithmetic of their planting) soon be going more or less all at once. That there was no greater variation in their ages and no ongoing planting is nobody's fault.

We are all surprised when apparently vigorous people die, regardless of age. We say, with some irritation, "Why, I saw him only yesterday. We had lunch together." We behave as though it was inconsiderate of him to die without telling us, and we are even more annoyed when someone else, a contemporary, does the same thing. It never seems to occur to us to develop replacement friendships in anticipation of the inevitable. Similarly, when there are enormous, rugged trees sheltering our homes—trees that, like our grandparents, have been there since before we were born—we do not think of planting new saplings. In any event, where could we plant them? The roots of the old trees run through the ground for yards, just as the lives of our elders run through our own, and the branches of the old trees shelter our homes as the love of our parents has sheltered our lives.

What we must do as these old patriarchs fall is to grub out the roots, fertilize the soil, and plant anew. We can remember them as we remember old friends, and be proud of them as we are of ancestors we never even saw, but we must be able to point out of the window to where a new generation is coming along.

The worst that can happen if all these old trees die is that our surroundings will for some years resemble those of our forebears 150 or 200 years ago. They started with nothing and so can we. While it now seems unlikely that elms can be used for replacements, this may actually be to our advantage; monoculture inevitably creates problems. What we should do as old trees pass is replace them with a mixture of other species, not just one, so that if disease attacks again our streets will not be denuded.

It is, of course, possible that a disease-resistant elm will be developed. There have already been some encouraging signs, but it is unlikely to duplicate the old elm in appearance. When a blight killed the American chestnut, the Chinese chestnut and some other hybrids were successfully introduced, but although they gave nuts they were borne on small trees resembling apples, not on timber trees like the old forest chestnut.

While I bow to no one in my admiration of the elm and consider it a great privilege to have lived to see them in their prime, I hope that if a disease-resistant type is developed it will not be planted as a solitary replacement. To do so would be to invite a recurrence of disaster. We live in a constantly changing world, not only socially but vegetatively. All we can do is look ahead and adapt our plantings to the situation. And while no new friend can take the place of an old one, replacement friendships can add to the enduring beauty of our lives.

Damn Popples

Along with "them damn popples" and puckerbrush, alders are considered hereabouts as among the most contemptible of plants. You can call them trees or shrubs as you prefer, but nobody likes them. Nobody but me, that is, and a few other long-time gardeners, who look upon all plants as useful in their place and treat alders with a sort of benign neglect. I don't think I would plant an alder—but I wouldn't take oath on it, because I have cultivated it's relatives: white birch, hazelnuts, and other members of the *Betulaceae*. On the whole though, there is no need to plant alders, because if there is a spot anywhere on your place that favors them they will plant themselves.

I have been itching to put the chain saw to some of ours all winter, but the snow has been so deep (about three feet) that if I could have got in to cut them the stubs would have been so high above the ground come spring I would have had to do the job all over. Then, after the snow went off (or some of it, because there are plenty of drifts left where I could cool a whole case of wine), the lane alongside which the alders grow was so soft I couldn't put a wheel on it. In consequence it is only now, past the middle of April, that the sound of the chain saw is heard in the land.

I am laying waste a twenty-foot swath of alders, ten feet on either side of a lane to the shore, because they are overarching the roadway so much they are beginning to rub against passing cars. When I made this road twenty years ago I cut all the alders on about four acres, leaving only gray birch and a few maples and spruce. Naturally the alders began their resurrection trick immediately (there is no keeping alders in the grave), and by now they are twenty feet tall and two feet in circumference. Each individual branch, that is, for they spring up like a shrub, half a dozen trunks spreading from the ground. We are leaving the tops to rot back as mulch but piling the heavier trunks back of the barn to dry; eventually they will be cut into stove lengths or little logs for a small fireplace.

I don't know that we do much with alder in this country, but in Europe it is used to construct inexpensive furniture and to make charcoal—although probably not as much as in days gone by, when charcoal was used in the recovery of iron from ore. I can remember being told as a boy that charcoal was used in the manufacture of gunpowder. I tried making it, but never succeeded in blowing myself up, so I suppose I didn't have the right formula. One thing I do remember is that the charcoal must be made from alders or willows. We had plenty of both, but the other ingredients (nitre and sulfur) were not so easily come by. The nitre was the problem. I could steal sulphur from the potting shed, where it was kept to dust roses, and there were also sulfur candles (real killers!) used to fumigate the greenhouse. Anyway, I was a succcessful charcoal burner, and I think I'll use some of my alders for that purpose. It should be better for one's health than those briquets of mysterious composition that one buys in the supermarket.

A funny thing about alders is that they are restricted, naturally, to the northern hemisphere—except in the Americas, where they grow as far south as Chile. Don't ask why because I don't know, and if anyone else does they have not, to my knowledge, published their findings. As we who live in New England know, alders prefer boggy places, but if they are unimpeded by obstructions they will work uphill from streams and ponds into quite dry conditions. I have a few growing in the sandy soil of my upper field, which is more suitable for cactus than semiaquatic plants, but their main forces are grouped in a patch of wild land below our shore pasture. That is where the twenty-footers live and have their being. They grow between and around great boulders covered with emerald moss, and even in midsummer a hole dug at their feet will soon fill with water. Skunk cabbages live in harmony with them, and a little later in the spring the ground closer to the road, where the sun shines briefly at midday, will be covered with dogtooth violets, some even thrusting their mottled leaves up through the gravel of the roadway.

It is a quiet place in the shade of the alders, reminding me of Hudson's *Green Mansions.* I have flown over the half million square miles of the Matto Grosso several times, and each time wondered what it would be like to be beneath that endless canopy of leaves rather than 25,000 feet above it. I am sure there is more life down there than is apparent from above. Even in my own small jungle, important events occur. I noticed this morning where a deer had crossed the road; it's cloven hoof marks showed deeply in the soft gravel, but there was no trail to be seen on the green, mossy carpet. A few years ago, a black duck had a nest in the stump of an old decaying spruce, just high enough to be above the wet ground. Ruffed grouse nest there frequently, and soon I shall hear the *Hylas,* the spring peepers. They frequent the pools between the boulders and the shores of the little fire pond beside my barn.

I think I shall take down just enough alders to clear the road and make some charcoal—gunpowder too, if I can get some nitre and the recipe. Old men living in the country never do really get old, except in years, and years are a mighty inexact yardstick.

War

By the Fourth of July the gardener feels that summer is finally here, and all is well with the world. The tomatoes are looking sturdy, the corn is coming, the beets and carrots are up, and he won't have to buy any plastic salad makings from the supermarket until November. All in all, he is feeling pretty satisfied with himself. He has even forgotten the cutworms that decimated the beet seedlings and lopped off the tomatoes, peppers, and eggplants. But pride goeth before a fall.

Four pests that can do more damage to a garden in a single night than all the cutworms, aphids and caterpillars, and bean and potato beetles in existence are deer, woodchucks, porcupines, and raccoons. (Of course, there are also rabbits, cats, dogs, and small children, not to mention the cyclones, windstorms, rain, hail, frost, drought, and other Acts of God that are visited upon us for our manifold sins and wickedness.)

The particular pest that afflicts one depends to a large degree upon where one gardens. The penthouse gardener is unlikely to suffer from the depredations of deer or porcupines, but cats, coming suddenly upon soft soil in which to establish sanitary facilities, will go out of their minds with joy. And English sparrows and starlings, no particular problem in the country, look upon young green sprouts on a rooftop as the Israelites beheld manna falling from heaven.

Although their gardens are bounded by paved roads and fences, suburbanites have long known that rabbits—supposedly inhabitants of a more rural scene—can clean out a row of lettuce overnight. They know, too, that rabbits are happy to build nests in which to raise more rabbits in gardens enclosed by houses on three sides and a railroad track on the fourth. And in recent years, raccoons have discovered that garbage in suburban refuse cans is just as tasty as that to be found in the country, and there is more of it.

Where I live, there is no pest on two, four, or any other number of legs that is is not waiting in the wings ready to assault whatever I grow. I have been able to keep deer out of my kitchen garden only by surrounding it with a six-foot-high pig-mesh fence, the interest on which investment probably exceeds the annual value of the produce it protects, but even this does not deter the coons. To a coon, six feet of wire fence is merely a jungle gym upon which it can work up an appetite before raiding the corn.

Last summer we stretched an electrically charged wire, the sort that is used to keep cows in a pasture, along the top of the fence. Were our raiders dismayed? I'll say not. In fact, I think they enjoyed being tickled. We then strung three more strands around the corn patch itself, which proved equally ineffective. Finally, we hung lighted oil lanterns on posts at the end of the rows. This did puzzle them for a few days, but then I think they figured we were just being considerate and lighting the night for them. We gave up and decided we would advise our guests (who are used to enjoying our frozen corn in midwinter) that, as the seedsmen often say, we had suffered a crop failure.

The only way I know to beat coons, and this goes for woodchucks too, is with a gun. The trouble with this method is that coons are nocturnal and groundhogs (woodchucks) are very early risers. Besides, in suburban areas, though not around here, the blast of a shotgun in the dark of night, or in the first faint light of dawning day, will bring all the police cars within five miles screaming into the neighborhood.

I merely mention this *en passant* because in the country, or in this part of Maine anyway, the sound of a gun or rifle between sunset and dawn just indicates that someone is jacking deer. Most of us never investigate such sounds of warfare. Who knows? One might run across a friend. Every time I hear a rifle shot I associate it with an unknown benefactor who is defending that part of my garden that is not fenced.

Porcupines can climb down fences, though they seldom do. They can climb up a forty-foot spruce with the greatest ease, and about the only way they can be prevented from completely killing a tree once they have started on it is by banding it with a three-foot strip of steel or aluminum. A couple of years ago porcupines decided they enjoyed a yellow willow near my barn, and before I took notice of what they were up to they had ripped it to pieces. After I banded it a branch still lived, a testament to the hold on life inherent in a willow, but it looks like something out of a picture of Belleau Wood or Guadalcanal.

If your garden is where porcupines can raid it, they will keep it as bare as the Sahara. I once knew a lady, a schoolteacher, who devoted most of her summers to internecine warfare with porcupines. It is said that the female is more deadly than the male, and if an example were needed she would provide it. After school closed each year Elizabeth came to her family farm in Maine, where she spent her summers. In the fullness of time small green things sprouted and grew, for Elizabeth was a first-rate gardener. But unhappily, and concurrently, porcupines appeared out of the woods.

It was a far stretch from the woods to the garden. Our pedagogue spent her summers, or most of them, on her back porch reading, knitting, drinking tea, and, because she was an ardent fisherwoman, thinking about the bass that had eluded her that morning but that she was sure she would catch for supper that night. During all of these sedentary musings she kept by her side a good, stout, battle-scarred two-by-three with one end whittled down to form a smooth handle for her delicate, schoolteacherly hand. She never wore shoes during the summer, perhaps because Diana is usually portrayed with her toes sticking out of sandals.

As soon as she noticed a "porky" emerge from the woods, she would keep him under strict surveillance until he had reached a point of no return in his journey toward the cabbage patch. At that moment, at that precise moment, she would light out, barefoot, skirts billowing behind her like those of a pioneer woman chasing an Indian who has stolen her child. Brandishing her club, she cut off the porky's retreat to the woods.

A porcupine's defense lies in its quills. It locomotes at about the same speed as a drunken man and with approximately the same gait. It is not built for speed. Elizabeth would stand, terrible in her wrath, and wait; when her prickly prey came in range she would fetch him a smart crack on the nose with her club, turn him over, and with her sharp little paring knife extract his liver and cut off his feet. The liver she ate, and the feet she delivered to the game warden to collect the porcupine bounty.

I don't know how many she disposed of during the course of a summer, but it must have been considerable. Come to think of it, perhaps her reason for going barefoot was to show her contempt for her victim. So far as I know, she never stepped on a quill and she was careful to stay out of range of the tail, which is what a porcupine will smite you (or your dog) with if you venture too close. Sadly for fiction, they cannot "shoot" their quills, which for those of us who inhabit their territory is just as well.

Not being geared to pursuing porcupines in my bare feet, I keep a .22 close at hand. When anyone sees a porky heading toward the garden he yells "Mark!" and I head off in a long reach to starboard and then come about on the other tack to head him off. When he is so close I can see the whites of his eyes, I shoot between them. If the bullet strikes a glancing blow from a distance, the porky's quills will deflect it, and you will have wasted your ammunition.

But I have forgotten the coons. A friend who had been having coon trouble (they had murdered twenty ducks he was keeping safely—he thought—in a pen) told me that the way to solve my problem was to buy a Havahart trap. Bait it, he said, with stinking fish or any old garbage, set it, and in the morning you will have caught something. He was quite right, but the difficulty is that what you catch may not be what you are setting your cap for.

There are other vagrants abroad at night besides coons. Sooner or later you are bound to find your neighbor's cat—or your own, if you have one—a prisoner. The cat will be indignant, but it won't have learned a thing. You are going to have to tally "cat" on your scoreboard regularly, unless or until the cat mysteriously disappears. Sometimes you will find larger game, say a skunk or a woodchuck, or even the coon you have been hoping for. The woodchucks and coons you can dispose of as your conscience allows. (My friend heaves them, trap and all, on the end of a line into the deepest part of his pond; when there are no more bubbles there is no more coon.) But a skunk is a different matter. Skunks present a problem that I have never been able to cope with. It has been my fixed habit to treat *Mephitis mephitis* with considerable respect. I suggest you turn the job over to someone lower on the ladder of seniority.

If you find it difficult to execute these night raiders as a matter of principle, lug them off and turn them loose where they can gorge themselves on someone else's garden, which they will ultimately do even if you think you have found a nice "woodsy" spot for them. They don't enjoy eating spruce trees and skunk cabbage any more than we do.

I must confess that I find it difficult to understand the logic of those who weep over a dead raccoon but employ paid assassins to work in the Chicago stock yards so that they can order "a sirloin, very rare, please," or enjoy the smell of a portion of dead pig roasting in the oven.

Well, each to his own. Pork and beans are pretty tasty too, but if you want any beans next winter you had better keep the woodchucks out of your bean patch.

George

Gardening is not just a hobby like collecting postage stamps or coins, or an exercise like golf or tennis, or a time-consumer like bridge or chess; it's a combination of healthful activity, artistic expression, and purposeful pursuit of knowledge. It truly does enrich the lives of those who practice it and it gives pleasure to the passer-by. Gardening is acknowledged as one of the great arts and is more difficult than most. Paintings remain unchanged as conceived by the artist and statues last almost forever unless physically destroyed, but even the finest gardens rarely outlive their makers. Even if they are spared by war and the elements, a few years' growth changes them beyond recognition, and the passage of a century sears them with old age and decay. They share with us a finite span of years, and it is perhaps this quality that makes the quiet of "grey old gardens" so appealing and sweetly sad and the memory of old gardeners so sweetly nostalgic.

In the olden days, when it was not considered demeaning to admit that you worked for a family in "domestic" employment, my grandfather kept a gardener who enjoyed his job, stayed at it most of his life, and in consequence made a modest but comfortable living. He had no desire to be socially or economically mobile, as it is called nowadays, and because his interests were relatively limited he gave all his thought to his job. As a result he was a superb gardener. I suppose he would have conceded that my grandparents were better off financially than he was, but it did not bother him, because if you are doing the job you enjoy most and are being adequately paid for it, you don't worry much about other peoples' position in life. He had another thing going for him: everyone in the village acknowledged his preeminence in his profession, which in itself is rewarding, and his employers accorded him the respect and friendship (properly distant, as they both wished) that his character and ability deserved.

THE GARDEN AND THE LAND

I can well remember the first time I met George, for that was his name. It is one of the very few things I can recall from so far back in my life. I cannot have been more than five years old, and it was during the time when I also first met my grandparents. They had picked me up only a few days earlier, an unknown grandson from a long way off who they were going to be saddled with for the next sixteen years. They were then in their sixties, and the thought of bringing up another child must not have been without its concerns.

I was inoculated with the gardening virus very early. The actual vaccination occurred when George, who had been digging with a sharp, square-tined English digging fork (this was long before the days of rototillers and other such aids to gardening), thrust the fork into the ground at the end of a row. Being as inquisitive and imitative as most children, I picked up the fork, but finding it too heavy to manage, I dropped it. One of the pointed tines pierced my right foot a little behind my third and fourth toes and left a wound sufficiently severe that a scar still remains. I have no recollection of pain, but starched linen and the smell of formaldehyde are still unfailing reminders of the occurrence. The stiff linen was inhabited by a nurse, who held me in her arms as we sat in the governess cart in which our fat little cob whirred us off to the doctor's office. The formaldehyde was, I suppose, what was used as an antiseptic in those days.

Some vaccinations don't "take," but there has never been any doubt of the efficacy of that one I administered to myself. My grandfather continued the job when he said, "George, take care of this boy and make a gardener out of him," or words to that effect. I must say that George did his best, and such of the art that comes to me as if I had been born with it is what he taught me.

It has been said that if you scratch an Italian you find a musician. It is equally true that if you scratch an Englishman you discover a gardener. I do not remember anyone in our village being without a garden. By garden, I do not mean a vegetable garden, though most had those too, but everyone grew a few flowers. Where an old row-house or cottage was slap up against the sidewalk there would still be tubs or pots of flowers on either side of the door, or perhaps a brick would have been removed from the paving next to the house so a climbing rose could grow there. One learned by exposure to a ministry of flowers.

I don't know just when George laid down the horticultural decalogue for me; I suppose it was over a period of time. The first rules must have been simple ones suited to my tender years, but collectively they became engraved in my memory like the marks of a chisel on an Egyptian temple wall. I know that now, when I do certain things or refrain from doing others, my actions are controlled by happenings of years long gone. I act not because I was taught so, as would a student recalling his instructor, but because I have a conditioned response.

I often think of a lecture George gave when visitors to the garden asked if a certain plant "liked" this or that. He had no truck with such nonsense. I am sure that he did not know the word *anthropomorphic,* but he might just as well have because he would say when someone had asked him, for example, whether brussels sprouts like heavy soil: "You'd think the bloody sprouts were people. Plants don't like things or dislike things; they just grow, and if you provide what they need, they do well, but if you don't, they'll be scrumpy and die. But they don't have feelings like you or me or Tiger." (Tiger was George's bull terrier pup.) While he didn't explain it to me, perhaps he could not have, his theory (which was fact) was that any brussels sprout liked the same things as any other brussels sprout—not at all like people, who may all be six-foot blonds with blue eyes, yet one will thrive on beef-steak and kidney pie while the next suffers indigestion on that diet.

George could go through a garden or greenhouse and tell without touching it whether a plant was doing well or poorly, and if the latter, what the trouble was. Some of it rubbed off on me. I wish more had, because growing plants successfully requires a symbiotic relationship that can only be achieved by companionship. Much can be learned from books, but it is impossible to come to that automatic relationship between man and plant without constant association.

Two things I learned about early were weeds and watering. We had several circular and crescent-shaped flower beds out on the lawn that were planted with calceolarias, ageratum, sweet alyssum, and the like. There must have been thousands of plants to be bedded out in the spring, and who better to do it than a small boy who could lie on a board on his abdomen and avoid treading down the bed. He could also lie on the same board to weed at a later date. There I learned bedding and weeding.

Watering is another art that can be acquired only by constant repetition and observation. Outdoors it is relatively simple because little harm can be done by over- or under-watering, but indoors or in a greenhouse it is not easy. You cannot water plants twice a week, or twice a day, or at any regular time. Time has nothing to do with it. The closest one

THE GARDEN AND THE LAND

could come to a universal rule would be to take each potted plant, immerse it in water until it is thoroughly soaked, and then not touch it again until the soil on top is dried out. What usually happens is that someone splashes around a little water every day as fast as possible and thinks the job is done. I have seen many potted plants where the soil on top was always moist but where the center of the ball of earth was bone dry. So many factors need to be considered: the size of the pot, type of pot, size of plant, type of plant, sunshine, humidity, soil—all play a part. A gardener can determine the need at a glance. George could.

I have made gardens all over the world wherever the opportunity presented itself, and a few times when one would have said it was quite impossible. I have gardened in England, not least of all in the gardens of friends, who never failed to impress me into service during country weekends because, "You love gardening so much." I have gardened in France, if gathering seed pods of "Flanders" poppies and scattering their contents around in other places can be considered gardening. I have tended garden in Mexico, where all I had to do was scratch a hole with my toe, insert a cutting, and keep it watered to have it grow. I have tilled the soil in half a dozen places in Pennsylvania, where apart from damage caused by bugs and summer heat, almost anything will thrive; and I have gardened in Brooklyn, New York, as well as Brooklin, Maine, and other places too numerous to recall. I have even planted seed and harvested a crop on board a ship in the middle of the Pacific Ocean, though my garden was a piece of flannel stretched across a bowl of water, and the crop was mustard and cress reaped with a pair of scissors. In fact, like most who are gardeners by choice and inheritance, I have never missed an opportunity to make two blades of grass grow where only one grew before, and thus, I hope, "deserve better of mankind and do more essential service to [my] country than the whole race of politicians put together."

Getting Away

When I was at home, I was in a better place.

— Shakespeare, *As You Like It,* Act II, scene iv

Mussels for Lunch

A little blue Volkswagen scurried up to the kitchen door this afternoon, skidded on the remains of the last snow, and stopped. A young lady got out, stuck her head in the door, and said, "Would you like some mussels?" She handed me a plastic ice cream bag heavy with dark blue shells, and without waiting for a reply, added, "I've got to hurry. I just gathered them this afternoon. G'bye."

The reason she did not wait for an answer was that the question was rhetorical. She knows I like mussels. I was grateful to her for scrambling over the ice floes until she could reach the rocks where the mussels cluster together as closely as peas in a pod. We ate them for lunch the next day with a glass of chablis, and they were superb.

Every time I say a word in praise of mussels I am fearful that I may initiate a run on them, rather like shouting "Oh how beautiful!" is supposed to have started an avalanche in the Alps. But, since I see that so scholarly a journal as *The Harvard Magazine* has publicly sponsored the mussel, and Harvard University Press has even published a mussel cookbook, written by Sarah Hurlburt (Cambridge, Mass., 1977), it's clear that the secret is out and there is no longer any point in maintaining silence.

Mussels, *Mytilus edulis,* abound on our shores. When the tide recedes every visible surface—mud, rocks, old shoes, waterlogged lobster traps, you name it—is encrusted with them. Surveying the shoreline, I am reminded of the passenger pigeons that once traveled in flocks so multitudinous that for mile after mile they darkened the sun. Then someone let the public in on their edibility and in a few short years they were gone—not just thinned out but vanished, every last single pigeon. I hope this does not happen to the mussel, but there is no telling. Mussels are so easy to harvest: you don't have to break your back, as you do digging clams. You don't need a lot of expensive gear, as you do to go lobstering or scalloping. In fact, you do not need anything but your hands, to pick the mussels off whatever they are fastened to, and a pail to put them in. They are anchored by a few threads called the byssus, the stuff usually referred to as the beard, which is what has to be cut off before you make your *moules mariniere*. There is no fisherman's luck involved in mussel "fishing." You don't have to come home smelling of strong drink with the truth not in you as do ordinary fishermen. (You can, of course, if you want to.) You can always get your limit, as long as you are not blind and are reasonably nimble. In fact, even a blind man could gather mussels if someone led him to the spot.

If there does develop a sudden enthusiasm for *Mytilus edulis,* I'll tell you one thing: it won't be sparked by the natives of the State of Maine. I have tried on a number of occasions to interest my local friends in mussels, but unless they want to placate me for some reason or other the response has been wholly negative. A young lady who works around here gathered a pail of magnificent mussels for me not long ago. They were enormous, about four inches long, and would have cost at least fifty cents apiece in Europe. When I had admired them sufficiently I asked her if she had ever eaten any. She looked at me stunned, as though I had gone out of my mind, and replied, "Wow. Well, I dunno. I tried *one* once."

I think the reason for the native attitude toward mussels is that they are so plentiful. The human mind is a strange assortment of prejudices, and one of the strangest is that it rejects those things that are easy to obtain or that do well without much help. At least that is so in America, where we have for generations lived pretty high off the hog. In Maine, lilacs grow in abandon around every deserted cellar hole, and while people break off great branches to bring indoors when they are in flower, they view them at other times with contempt, saying, "Them damn things. You can't kill 'em." Well, perhaps not, but I have yet to see anything that cannot be destroyed by the hand of man.

Having lived here and there around the world I have seen real poverty and real hunger, and have become increasingly irritated by the politicians and bureaucrats who constantly talk about our starving Americans. I have not seen many of them. Few in this fortunate country are hungry, and if they are it is often because they have such rigid dietary habits that they would rather go hungry than eat something unfamiliar. As long as the supply of hot dogs, hamburgers, and french fries holds out they are happy, but were you to suggest they eat rabbit (another source of protein that can be raised quickly) or mussels, they would riot.

Graham Hurlburt, director of administrative services at Harvard, another mussel enthusiast, says that it is theoretically possible to raise as much as 43 billion pounds of mussel meat a year in a water area of about 16.5 square miles. A ton a meat a year for every person on earth. Such estimates have a way of becoming cockeyed when put into practice, but even making intelligent use of what we have growing naturally would make a substantial contribution to our food supply. However, being as stupid as we are, we shall probably poison our coastal waters. In the meantime, there would seem to be no need for anyone to starve.

Unfortunately, mussels are rarely offered for sale in inland towns, but if you live where you can obtain them almost any good cookbook has a recipe for mussels *mariniere,* which seems to be the basic method of preparation. It is one that we employ often. We have, however, a few more elegant ones. One that you might like is:

ELEGANT MUSSELS

Obtain however many mussels you want, the larger the better. For every two dozen mussels, you'll need a medium-sized onion, a good-size carrot, a celery stalk (leaves and all) cut up, three-quarters of a cup of white wine, and the same amount of water. For topping, a three-inch strip of bacon for each mussel and some grated Romano cheese.

Scrub the mussels well and remove the beards. If you do not know where the mussels come from, or if they were from a sandy or muddy spot, let them stand in a pail of cold water overnight, preferably salt water. If you picked them off a rock or piling you probably won't have to go through this stage, as the purpose is to allow them to disgorge whatever sand may be in the shell.

Steam the mussels for six minutes in all the ingredients except the bacon and cheese. If you have a *bouquet garni* around you can throw that in the pot too. Stir once—no more, or the meat may fall out and you'll have to retrieve it from among the shells. When the shells are open, at the end of the six minutes, take one shell off each mussel and leave the meat in the other half. Put a strip of bacon and a shake of cheese on each mussel and shove them under the broiler until the bacon begins to brown. Serve as a first course or as an hors d'oeuvre and thank God you don't have any silly ideas about not eating mussels.

The liquid in which the mussels have been cooked should be strained off and used as one would clam broth. If you are making *moules mariniere,* the liquid should be thickened slightly with a roux of butter and flour and poured over the mussels, shells and all, when they are served, preferably in deep soup dishes.

A Great Plague

I have always had a sympathy for parsons. In some respects, the job of the preacher is easier than that of a weekly columnist, for he has, in the Bible, a variety of ideas already to hand. If he cannot think of a subject any other way, he can use the time-honored approach of closing his eyes and putting a finger on an open page and learning what the Lord has to say. Of course he may be directed to the Begats, which would give him a spot of trouble, but on the other hand he may light on one of those grim Old Testament texts, such as Chronicles II, XXI, verses 14 and 15, that reads: "Behold, with a great plague will the Lord smite thy people, and thy children, and thy wives, and all thy goods:/ And thou shalt have great sickness by disease of thy bowels, until thy bowels fall out by reason of the sickness day by day," which is enough to scare any backslider into returning to the fold.

I speak with some authority on this subject, having spent a fair amount of time in the tropics where one is quite apt to be smitten with "great sickness of the bowels"— a smiting not soon to be forgotten. I can recall with some clarity being in the small hillside town of Taxco in Mexico with an old friend (now passed to a more sterile, if not better world) who was so afflicted. He felt the need of a doctor so I found one for him, a German physician who spoke little of either Spanish or English. He said, after my friend had described his symptoms (which were rather obvious), that he would have to take out his intestines, which was as close as his knowledge of English permitted him to come in prescribing a cathartic. The patient shuddered and replied that it would be impossible, as his bowels had already fallen out.

On the other hand, while the preacher has the Bible to refer to, he has less catholicity of subject than the columnist. This columnist, anyway, who, though he is labeled a garden writer, is allowed by understanding editors to vault the fence and treat the whole world as his garden.

When I arose this morning I knew I had to produce a column to meet a deadline. I had been thinking about it for an hour before I dragged myself out of bed. I had concluded that I would have to be guided by those sage words of Doctor Johnson that have overcome the indolence of many a writer: "A man may write at any time if he will set himself *doggedly* to it."

I bathed and shaved with extra care, having been taught that "Manners myketh man" and a tidy appearance is good discipline in itself. Of course, I had to delay a few minutes before breakfast to learn from television what new disasters had overtaken the world while I slept. The most important news seemed that Americans could, as of 12:01 last night, legally own gold. As I have neither the funds nor the inclination to stock up on gold, this concession on the part of my rulers did not seem to be worth all the fuss that was being made about it.

Breakfast, consisting of half a grapefruit and a slice of toast, was disposed of briefly. However, just as I was setting myself to be dogged, a neighbor came to the kitchen door and told me one of our ewes was loose and standing in the middle of the road. He had tried to corral her for me but had been unsuccessful. I said out loud, "Oh damn," but secretly rejoiced in an excuse to delay a little longer. It turned out to be longer than anticipated, but with a handful of grain I was finally able to entice the ewe back into the pasture. In the process, though, I noticed that the catch on the gate had shaken loose, which was why she had been able to escape, so of course I had to get a hammer and a hatchet and a few nails from the barn. Having obtained these and secured the gate, I felt it would be wise to "make assurance double sure," so I retraced my steps and got a couple of lengths of binder twine from where we hang it when we open bales of hay. Good, now I would write.

On my way back to the house, "the whining schoolboy, with his satchel, and shining morning face, creeping like a snail unwillingly to school," I suddenly remembered I had not watered the plants in the greenhouse, The day was sunny, so obviously they would be in trouble if not attended to promptly; attend to them I must, I had no choice. But having done so, I picked a few dead leaves off the geraniums and admired the amaryllis and Christmas cactus, for, after all, there is not much point in having a greenhouse if one cannot take a minute to admire what is in it. Now, I would get to my typewriter.

Just as I came into the shed, Helen called to me, "The mail just came. Why don't you go to the box and get it before you take off your coat?" Naturally one must take time to look at the mail, for is it not delivered at great risk of life and limb by those swift couriers who allow neither sleet nor snow, or whatever, to deter them from the swift completion of their appointed rounds? After perusing it, and consigning most of it unopened to the wastebasket, time had come for morning coffee. While I was enjoying this, Helen suddenly asked, "Have you got your piece done yet?" To which I replied indignantly, "How could I, you know I've been busy every minute since I got up!"—an excuse she ignored completely, saying unfeelingly, "Well, you'd better get busier if you expect to get it out in the mail today."

So I did.

The Truth About Lobsters

Some years ago, when I was visiting friends in Pennsylvania, I was taken to dine at a local restaurant that was making a name for itself. My friends, thinking to do something nice for a visiting fireman from Down East, suggested that I have lobster, which, they claimed, was excellent. Now I make it a rule, not quite inviolable but close to it, never to eat a lobster away from the State of Maine. This was one of the times that I slipped, and it taught me not to do so again. I was so busy talking to my hostess I did not hear my host give the order, which I subsequently learned was for lobster tails. At that time these were not as commonly found on menus as they are today, and I had not previously made their acquaintance, so when my order was served I was puzzled. My host, seeing my hesitation, asked if there was anything wrong, to which I replied, "Where's the rest of it?" and then added, "You know, the front end—the body and the claws."

I soon learned, of course, that there was no front end and that what I had been given was what is known as a South African lobster tail. There were a couple of things wrong. In the first place, I'll trade anyone the tail of a lobster for the body and claws; all the best and tastiest and most tender meat, not to mention the tomally, are in the bow end. The other thing that bothered me was that my lobster had obviously departed this life before it had been cooked. The tail of a live lobster curls up as tight as a sow bug and stays that way after it is boiled, and a sure sign of a dead one is for it to lay out flat like the specimen on my plate. Anybody who lives east of Cape Cod has been taught from childhood that the surest and most agonizing way to commit suicide is to eat a lobster that was dead when it was put in the pot.

However, as my host assured me that he had eaten dozens of South African lobster tails and had survived I had, for politeness's sake, to taste it. I did, and can report that I suffered no ill effects, but it is no more like lobster than a lobster is like a pork chop. I still don't know what the South Africans do with the front end; there has to be something up there, the tails don't crawl around without some guidance from the bridge, but whatever it is, it is not equipped like a lobster. I suspect they are nothing but oversized ocean-going crawdaddies.

On the same menu was a combination called "Turf and Surf." Inquiry elicited the information that this was a filet mignon and a "lobster" tail served on the same plate. Now, although I count myself catholic in my dietary preferences, I view the consumption of fish and meat together akin to putting chocolate ice cream on oysters. Since the lobster was not a lobster anyway I let it pass, but had I witnessed the marriage of a Maine lobster to a piece of steer meat I would have felt a protest was due to uphold the honor of my homeland.

I admit to being a trifle spoilt when it comes to lobsters. Although I have better sense than to tend any traps of my own, even a few, there are, in season, always a dozen or so buoys bobbing around a few hundred feet off my shoreline. If I want a couple of lobsters all I have to do is tell some local lobsterman the night before I need them.

The whole essence of good lobster eating lies in getting your victim while he is still vigorous and salty, while he still can—and will, if the plugs come out—snap off your finger. When I pass through airports I avoid, if I am able, passing the depressing corner where a bored-looking woman is sitting behind a tank of comatose crustaceans that, if they are still in this world, are within a breath of the next.

Certainly the best place to eat a lobster is on the shoreline on the coast of Maine, preferably al fresco, on the rocks, and if not there, then in one of the many "Lobster Pounds" or "Lobster Pools" that operate during the summer. The best way to cook a lobster is by boiling or steaming, and the only approved way to eat one is to put on your old clothes, roll up your sleeves, and tear it limb from claw.

There is a difference of opinion about the cooking procedure. The tender-hearted advocate a large pot filled with scalding water into which the flapping sacrifice is thrust head on, thus, it is said, terminating its life suddenly and painlessly. Most lobster pools operate on this principle, not that they worry too much about the lobster's feelings, but because it is safer and faster and simpler for them when they are cooking hundreds of orders to just stuff the lobsters into a mesh bag and drop them into the bubbling cauldron, head or feet first, as they come.

The other school, to which I belong, maintains that the most succulent lobster is one that has been cooked in a minimum of water. This is particularly true of shedders, that is to say, the lobster that is changing his old coat of armor for a better fitting one. If shedders are cooked in a tub full of water they come out looking like a man who has just been fished out of the ocean and stands with the brine running out of his pants' legs into his squelchy shoes. The proper way to do the job is to take a large smoky old black pot, such as the one we have hanging in the shed, and pour no more than a pint of sea water into it. Next come the lobsters (our pot holds about a dozen), which should be packed in like sardines, and on top of them should be placed six inches of fresh rockweed. It won't hurt if you drop a few dozen clams on top of the rockweed before you put on the lid. And if your lobsters seem particularly muscular, they may be weighted with a rock.

By the time you have accomplished the foregoing, one of your assistants will have the fire burning; on this, suitably braced so that it won't fall over and extinguish the blaze, you place the kettle. If you are the type whose heart bleeds for the pain and anguish of all God's creatures, you walk swiftly out of earshot, and finding a comfortable rock, seat yourself thereon and sip a boilermaker while the statutory cooking time passes. (For the benefit of those of this refined age who have missed the more vulgar pleasures of yesteryear, a boilermaker is a shot of bourbon and a beer chaser. About four of these at suitable intervals will carry you comfortably through a lobster cookout.)

Although I have never seen a resident of this state eat a lobster other than boiled, whether *au natural* or in a stew or salad, there are those, usually city folks from "away," who go in for the more exotic forms of cookery, such as stuffed broiled lobster; lobster *à l'Americaine,* which isn't American at all and involves chopping a live lobster into serving pieces, which are then sautéed in oil and flamed in cognac;

GETTING AWAY

lobster thermidor; lobster Cantonese; and lobster Savannah, to name but a few. This latter dish is a production of Lock Ober's Cafe in Boston, an institution that endears itself to the thinning ranks of the male chauvinists by refusing to admit women to the ground floor of their ancient restaurant. I have sat there of a snowy winter evening, watching the ladies about to be guided upstairs by their escorts peering in the steamy windows at the shining domes of the silver covers on the counter and the jovial customers washing down their oysters with a stein of ale, for all the world like characters from a Dickens Christmas story.

The fancy lobster recipes originated in more sophisticated surroundings than we find around here, places where diners are embarrassed by eating with their fingers, the only way one can successfully handle a boiled lobster. I had a very uppercrust lady visit me once. She said that she liked lobsters, so I told her to put on her old clothes and I would take her to a lobster joint nearby. I was a bit shocked when she showed up in a tweed skirt, an angora sweater, and a silk scarf around her head, with about five thousand dollar's worth of diamond rings on her beautifully manicured hands. She looked apprehensive when the steam from the boiling lobster kettles enveloped her on the way into the restaurant, and more so when the waitress, after rather sketchily wiping off the bare wooden table, placed a fragrant, two-pound lobster in front of her. She attacked it at first with her knife and fork, which is about equivalent to attempting to break into Fort Knox with a can opener, but soon decided that she was not going to get anywhere that way. She turned to me and said, "O.K. Roy, you win. How do you do it?"

There are several ways to eat a boiled lobster; I gave her my version, which is to first take off the legs and suck them out. That done, you break off the tail and open the body so that you can scoop out the tomally and pick out the body meat. The best part of the lobster, the claws and the knuckles, come next. I leave the tail, which is the toughest, until last, so that if I get stuck I have had all the best. I seldom get stuck. My friend watched and listened carefully, and, being a good sport despite her Park Avenue looks, took off her rings, rolled up her sleeves, put on a bib, and dug in. She admitted later that it was the best lobster she had ever eaten.

Years ago, when I was young and impecunious (now I am neither young nor poor, which is about as disadvantageous as my former state), I lived near Rockport, Maine, where there was an establishment that cooked and packed lobsters for shipment up to Boston. Although it was a secret kept from the summer people, I learned that if you got there at the right time you could buy lobster knuckles for twenty-five cents a pound. The reason they were sold locally was because it would have cost more to pick out the meat than they could get for it. For me it was like finding El Dorado in the back yard. Knuckles do not weigh very much, the shell part, that is, so for a dollar I could get a big bowl of the tenderest lobster meat. I will admit that they were a bit of a nuisance to pick, but my time was not worth much anyway. All I did with the meat was place it it in a skillet with a generous portion of butter, some pepper, and salt, and after a few minutes over a low flame I had a dish beyond compare.

Because they don't know anything about the mores of New England, or anyway the older and more rural parts of it, the bleeding heart brigade in our nation's capital have an idea that Maine is a depressed area. They are not accustomed to people who "make do" as a matter of principle, and think that they must be in direst poverty, particularly when said paupers line up to get all the free handouts that any fool is willing to give them.

I mention this as a preamble to an illustrative incident that occurred one afternoon when I was on my way home with a bag of knuckles. Passing the only hardware store in town, I remembered that I wanted a hammer. I went in and hefted a couple, and finding one that I liked I took it to the clerk. Then, the odor of my lobsters reminding me, I said, "Charlie, do you have any nutcrackers around?" He looked at me for a minute and asked, "What do you want them for?"

In more sophisticated parts of the country the storekeeper will, if you ask for a pair of nutcrackers, either get them or say he doesn't have any. Not in Maine. Charlie looked at me for another minute or so before he addressed himself to the problem. He had, by this time, discovered what I had in the bag and guessed my purpose. "Hell, " he said, "You just bought a hammer. Ain't you got any rocks on your place?" (An idle question in Maine.) "Don't be wastin' your money." I didn't. I went home and cracked my lobster knuckles on a granite boulder outside the kitchen door in the warm afternoon sunshine.

Alas, the days of lobster knuckles at twenty-five cents a pound are long gone, but if I eat lobster less frequently than I once did I enjoy it just as much, and have learned that singing "Backward, turn backward, O Time, in your flight," doesn't get you a thing.

GETTING AWAY

Things I Miss

People frequently ask me if I don't find life in the country dull and miss the excitement of the city. After years of fielding the question with the answer that I am a contented man, I finally came to the conclusion that I would have to find something I miss in order to placate my questioners. So, I did some hard thinking and found that there *are* a few things I miss—but I doubt they are the ones my friends had in mind. They are not museums and libraries and theaters, nor the sophisticated society my friends are concerned about. People would be surprised at the background of some of those who live quietly here on the coast of Maine, supremely uninterested in wider company. No, the things I miss are so simple they seem of no importance compared to the Boston Symphony and the Metropolitan Opera Company.

One thing I miss is having my shoes shined, At ten o'clock every morning in my city office there would come a knock at the door and a soft Italian voice would ask if I wanted a shine. The owner of the voice was a dark-skinned Sicilian, a first-generation immigrant who never had learned to speak English very well. He was old and bent and had so many patches on the knees of his trousers that they formed pads for him to kneel on. He could shine shoes so well that after his ministrations you could be blinded by them in bright sunlight. He lived in an Italian neighborhood in South Philadelphia in a little brick house exactly like row upon row of other little brick houses. He owned it and was very proud of it and kept it spotless. After I had known him for about twenty years, one day (having learned that I was a gardener) he asked me if I would like to see his fig tree. It was beautifully espaliered on the back of his house, and flourishing. In the winter he covered it with old gunny sacks to protect it. He sat me in a chair made from half a barrel, where I could see the fig tree, and gave me a glass of his homemade wine. I have drunk better wine, but he welcomed me as another gardener, and that was what counted. I miss him.

Another thing I miss from my city days, though not so personally, are the hat cleaning and shoe repair shops. The corner stores were often tobacconists with wooden Indians by the door. There was a chain of such shops, each with its floor on a level with the sidewalk. (The owners maintained that even one step kept people out.) The hat and shoe establishment was usually nearby. I can still hear the hiss of steam as the hats were being blocked, and the rattle of the pulleys on the shaft of the machine where the cobblers were working. Everything was quite unhurried, although you could get new heels—soles too, for that matter—on your shoes while you waited. It was nice to climb the two steep steps onto the shoeshine stand and sit there inhaling the odors of shoe paste, leather, and cleaning fluid. There was always a paper some previous client had left that you could glance at if you wished. When the man with the brushes placed your foot on the little steel rest, shaped like Robinson Crusoe's man Friday's footprint, he took your ankle in his hand; I can still remember its warmth, as I can the three or four sharp cracks of the polishing cloth signaling that the job was done.

I suppose there are no longer any hat cleaning establishments, as men more often go bareheaded. In the city of my memory there were several men's hat shops just as there were milliners for the ladies. For men, Stetson's was *the* place to go. They had an immense stock of hats in many colors and sizes, all carefully stacked, one inside the other, behind glass or in deep drawers. The salesman would place on your head an oval device resembling some medieval instrument of torture, and after tightening it would announce that you needed size seven and a quarter, or whatever. The color and size determined, finer adjustments would be made on a stretching device. I always had a haircut before buying a hat. The hat would stretch as your hair grew, but if fitted to a full head of hair would drop around your ears after a haircut.

The hat cleaning establishments flourished because the investment of ten dollars for a Stetson envisioned at least three years' use. Normally I left my hat to be cleaned on the way to work and retrieved it on the way home, wearing an old hat I kept in the office if I had to go out during the day so I would not be conspicuous.

Shoe shines and hat cleanings were, at one time, part of the life of many city people, but I suppose they are no longer available in the city or elsewhere. Cities were different when I began to work in them sixty years ago, different even from when I left them twenty years ago. Of course, my point of view has changed too. I think, though, that the cities have changed more than I. Most men now living who are less than forty years old have no idea at all about what big cities were like even twenty years ago, let alone fifty. The general opinion seems to be that they were old fashioned, inefficient, and dirty, and that the people who occupied them lived incredibly deprived lives without all the modern electronic gadgets. How could they have managed without television, computers, radio, hi-fi, quick frozen food, supermarkets, interstate highways, fast food outlets, trans-oceanic airplanes, nuclear power, oil heat, mechanical refrigeration, power mowers, Agent Orange—but why go on, the list is endless. I think everyone would concede, though, that there was better public transportation; they would have to, because public transportation today (except by air, which is much less comfortable than travel by rail) is almost nonexistent.

Apart from specifics, what I think of as our greatest loss is that although we worked just as hard twenty years ago, the pace was more leisurely. People were more satisfied to make a pleasant living and let it go at that. There was no great desire to sacrifice everything to "advancement" and then come to the end of a career short of the goal—for there never is a "top" anyway. There were fewer giant corporations. Most were small by today's standards, and a great many firms were privately owned or partnerships, where the owners took pride in being possessed of a detailed knowledge of every phase of the business and conducted it on a personal basis. I am told amalgamations are a trend of the times, and I do not dispute it, but I believe much of our social injustice today arises from people not knowing each other well enough. It is easy to view those who are employed in a large business as "workers" and the superiors as faceless management. It is less easy when firms are small or broken down into units where each employee has at least a speaking acquaintance with and responsibility for the other.

In New York in those days there was a chain of restaurants, maybe three or four, that operated on an honor system. One was close to the corner of Park Avenue and 42nd Street. It was called the Exchange Buffet. They were cafeterias in which the customer helped himself at a long, attractive food counter where little signs gave the price of each dish. He then carried his food to a table and ate lunch, and on the way out told the cashier how much he owed. I asked the manager if most people were honest. He answered, "We have no way of knowing, but we think so. Our prices are modest and we make a nice profit, so I guess they must be." I wonder if they are still in business. If they are, they are one of the things I miss about the city.

Vacation Time

When I was driving into Ellsworth, the county seat, not long ago to buy some grain for a flock of Cornish hens that rapidly were approaching the age when fate, in the form of a sharp cleaver, would overtake them, I narrowly missed being obliterated by a "recreational vehicle" about the size of a Greyhound bus. It was speeding downhill into town and the driver apparently did not see the YIELD sign cautioning against entering traffic. While I was, as the kids say, "shook up," I did not hold it against the driver of the camper, as he was on the main highway and was unlikely to expect that a rather insignificant side road had the right of way.

During the tourist season I travel as infrequently as possible, for the roads are crowded with cars bearing foreign license plates driven by people all hurrying to get somewhere other than where they are. Each year the traffic gets worse, and it is next to an impossibility to escape from any of the several shopping centers after one has succeeded in getting in. As recently as twenty years ago there were no shopping centers in Ellsworth, and while there was more traffic in the summer than in the winter, there were no recreational vehicles and not many trailers. Visitors came in their sedans, or occasionally old touring cars, and either stayed with friends or put up for the night in the relatively few motels or more frequent tourist homes. There were also accommodations in a few old-fashioned summer hotels, which were still operating back then. Anyway, nobody carried his bed on his back—or on wheels behind.

Thirty years ago, trains were still hauling passengers, although to be truthful the railroads were staggering and almost on the ropes. When I was a young man I rode trains on all extended trips, as did most other people. I owned a car and can remember a few trips by road that seem in retrospect to be glamorous, but I doubt I would think them so if I had to repeat them today.

My first trip by rail to New England was made in 1926. I can remember boarding the train in New York's Grand Central Station in the evening, headed for a vacation in Vermont. It was a long train, composed of a number of sleeping cars, a smoking car and lounge, two dining cars, and half a dozen day coaches. The porter, who in those days was "colored" and not "black," showed me my upper berth and took my bag, then brushed my straw boater, placed it in a paper bag, and deposited it ceremoniously in one end of the little hammock designed to hold various personal odds and ends while the passenger slept. The berths being already made up, there was nowhere to sit except in the lounge car or the washrooms, so, like most of my fellow passengers, I went to bed.

The only bedrooms in these early Pullman cars were at either end, next to the washrooms. The men's room was at one end of the car and the women's at the other, the remainder of the space being occupied by upper and lower berths. If you did not have a bedroom, which only plutocrats could afford, the next best thing was an entire section, which meant that the upper berth was not lowered and you could sit up in bed without knocking out your brains. If you could not afford a section you could reserve a lower, if you got your bid in early enough. This relieved you of the need to climb, which you had to do if all you could afford was an upper, which is what I usually had.

When you were ready to retire, the porter brought along his ladder and assisted you into your aerie. Theoretically, if you had a sudden urge to escape in the middle of the night you rang a bell and the porter reappeared with the ladder. In real life, however, your summons was not always attended to promptly; the porter could be asleep, helping someone else, shining shoes, visiting in the next car, or answering any of half a dozen other demands on his time. In such a case, all you could do was slide out, holding onto the edge of the berth and hoping that nobody would come along to witness your naked flesh as your pajama top or tee shirt parted company with your pants. I don't know what happened to nonagenarians with arthritis. I guess if they could not get a lower they stayed home.

Getting dressed or undressed in an upper berth required skill that could only be acquired after a long apprenticeship. You could take off your jacket and vest (we all wore vests then) in the aisle and place them on hangers attached to the curtains that separated your berth from the gaze of the vulgar, but removing your pants was another matter. If you did not mind being seen in your stockinged feet you removed your shoes before you climbed the ladder. It was not easy, because you had nowhere to sit. If you took them off in your berth you lay on your back, pulled your knees as close to your chest as your belly would allow, and, after struggling with recalcitrant knots, got them off and slipped them into a little bag, also in the curtain, from which the porter would remove them during the night to shine.

The real trick was to get out of your pants. As an old upper berth veteran I knew that the best way to escape them was to assume a fetal position, undo the fly buttons (no zippers in those days), elevate your hips an inch, and slide the waistband down to where, when you rolled on your back again, you could shove them below your knees. Getting them on in the morning called for about the same contortions in reverse. Of course if it was winter and you were wearing long-handled underwear (and didn't give a damn), you stripped down to these underpinnings in the aisle and did your best to get behind the curtains before you were approached by some shuddering female who sidled past you with averted eyes.

While the two superdeluxe bedrooms at the ends of the car had their own toilet and lavatory facilities, all the rest of the passengers used the general washrooms. It sometimes got to be a bit of a scramble if a couple of dozen men wanted to ablute at the same time in the four washbasins and one john the establishment afforded, but somehow it worked out. There was a leather-covered settee in the washroom where you could wait your turn, and if that was occupied you could just stand in the aisle. I cannot remember anyone ever getting very distressed about it. That was the way things were, and I suspect we were more tolerant of minor inconveniences in those days.

Travelers varied in the seriousness of their ablutions. Some merely dabbed a little water on their faces, combed their hair, and straightened their ties, but there were others I always surveyed with wonder and admiration. They appeared in bathrobes, carrying overnight bags. They took their time, stripped to the waist, had what amounted to a sponge bath, shaved, slapped eau de cologne on their faces, dropped their pajamas, donned clean white underwear and shirts, repacked their bags, and retired, leaving us less formal characters feeling as though we were bums who had been sleeping in a boxcar.

In one particular all travelers were alike, and that was in the care they took to leave the washbasin clean and shining. The ritual was, after you had dried your face and hands, to carefully clean the basin and dry it with your towel. Not to have done so would have offered *prima facie* evidence that you were an oaf, bereft of good manners, and it was remarkable how infrequently one met people of this type. I suppose that even the first-time traveler watched those ahead and emulated them. I wish I could say as much of moderns in airplane washrooms, which are frequently left in deplorable condition.

My 1926 trip was to a summer establishment that is still operating,

GETTING AWAY

and, I believe, under the management of the same family. It is the Basin Harbor Lodge near Vergennes, Vermont. It has been substantially modernized over the years, but when I was there it consisted of the main hotel and some small cottages on the shore of Lake Champlain. Guests coming from the New York area traveled, as I did, on the night train, arriving in Vergennes early in the morning. They were met by the original owner who, as I recall him, was an old man even then. He drove an enormous Pierce-Arrow touring car, and after loading his passengers aboard (their bags came later, by horse and wagon), he proceeded at high speed to Basin Harbor along a narrow, curving, dirt road, leaving a plume of dust towering behind. A peculiarity of those early touring cars was that they were, or appeared to be, innocent of stabilizers. As a consequence, passengers occupying the back seat were hurled from side to side on every curve. I owned one, a Flint, and on any trip of length my rear passengers got carsick.

All I did at Basin Harbor, and all that any guests did at summer hotels, for that matter, was to relax, go on picnics, talk to other guests (there were always some pretty girls), eat, read, fish in the lake, or play golf. I remember buying honey to take home; a local farmer sold it for twenty-five cents a comb or five for a dollar. Happy days.

I never went back to Basin Harbor nor, for that matter, to many other summer hotels, but they remain a fragrant memory. There are few left, and they will soon be a thing of the past. It is nothing that they have done that causes their demise, but rather changing patterns of social conduct. As late as the 1930s, families took vacations together, staying for their two weeks, or longer if their employment and pocketbooks permitted, at large, rambling, usually frame, hotels. They did not have to go anywhere else to be entertained. Everything was "on the house," or, if not free, available for a modest additional charge.

Some of these places were pretty snooty, like the Mountain View House in Whitefield, New Hampshire, or the Crawford House at Crawford Notch. Dinner jackets in the evening and formality at all times was expected except when actually in the pool or on the tennis court. And even on the tennis court, heavy white flannel trousers and shirts were *de rigueur*. At the smaller summer vacation homes that were less expensive, a pretty formal code of conduct was still maintained. There were no signs hanging out tolling one in with the invitation "Come as you are." Of course, they were "segregated," but nobody except those kept out thought much about it. Negroes were no problem because they never tried to crash the gate and probably couldn't afford to anyway. Jews were a special problem, because they could afford to pay the tab, and, through a strange oversight of the Lord, quite often looked and behaved like Christians. They were usually identified by a whispering campaign and found that either the hotel was full or the only rooms left available were in an annex. Despite these unpleasant facts the summer hotels were, for those who could patronize them, exceedingly comfortable and happy places to stay.

Perhaps when the world runs out of gasoline, people will turn again to summer hotels and to trains. Sometimes it takes a complete breakdown, a "nervous collapse," to bring a man to his senses. One hopes it will also bring him to his senses racially; *quien sabe,* it seems to be trending that way.

Here Yesterday, Gone Today

It grieved me to read not long ago that the Pullman Company will not be building railroad cars any more. I think perhaps I was particularly stricken because I had devoted most of my business life to aiding and abetting the airlines, which share responsibility with the automobile for the destruction of rail passenger travel.

The matter continued to trouble me, for I soon realized that in addition to contributing to the downfall of the railroads, and thus to that of the Pullman Company, I had been an accessory to a much greater sin. That was the complete and utter destruction of the fleet of magnificent and luxurious ocean liners that saw their blossoming and death during my own generation. The only good thing to be said about their departure is the fact that they died and were buried in the twinkling of an eye. They did not linger on, like Amtrak, to rub salt in our wounds. One day they were here, with passengers and stevedores crowding the Hudson River piers, with the neatly jacketed stewards taking our hand luggage and showing us to our staterooms, with messengers carrying last-minute telegrams and fruit and flowers and champagne through the high wall of riveted steel that was the ship's side—and then, suddenly, they were gone.

The piers where these leviathans docked are still there. They are like empty tombs, cold, enormous, and awe-inspiring—monuments built by a past civilization, like the pyramids. Along New York's 12th Avenue, from about 14th Street to 60th, is where these North Atlantic monsters paused to load and discharge between voyages. The proud names of the owners—the Cunard Line, the Holland America Line, the French Line, the Hamburg Amerika Line, the United States Line, and others—were once emblazoned on the barnlike ends of the piers. Some are still there, but the glory is gone.

Flying to Europe is merely transporting your body from one side of the Atlantic to the other. It is accomplished in a few hours. The trip itself is nothing. Young travelers of today who have never crossed the ocean except by air have not the slightest notion of the unhurried pleasure, the space, and the luxury provided by ocean liners. Not even the finest hotels could compete with them in the comfort and attention they offered their clients.

A measure of the quality of the service afforded aboard the great ships is evidenced by a story told me by the chief steward of one of the "Queens," I forget which one. He said that for many years, until her death, in fact, an elderly lady had retained a suite aboard his ship and occupied it continuously except for the time the ship went in for her annual overhauling. While there was no question that her mode of life was eccentric and expensive, she claimed that she could not duplicate the luxury and personal service anywhere else in the world for the price. On the ship she had a resident doctor; stewards and maids were as close as her call bell twenty-four hours a day; she had available the most superb cuisine, with meals in the dining saloon or in her cabin, as she chose; she could receive or send telegrams, or telephone anyone, just as she could had she been ashore; and she had complete privacy, if she wished, or the company of some of the most interesting people in Europe or on the American continent when she desired.

Compare this, if you will, with being cramped into an aluminum box and hurled across the Atlantic in a few hours. Far from wanting to stay aboard for pleasure, you can't wait to escape, only to find yourself in the chaos and discomfort and confusion of a modern airport. By contrast, when one arrived at Southampton by sea on a liner that might be carrying many more passengers than even the largest jet of today, everything went smoothly.

I have had a good deal of experience with both modes of travel. I made my first trip eastbound across the Atlantic as a very small boy in

1902, and have crossed many times since. My first trip by air was on a "pregnant" Pan American Boeing in 1949. (Pan-Am made its first commercial flight from New York to Portugal via the Azores ten years earlier, in 1939.) The great passenger steamers—*Queen Mary, Normandie, Rotterdam, United States, Queen Elizabeth*—were the unchallenged rulers of the Atlantic until after World War II and kept going for another twenty years. Then suddenly, when the jets got into the transoceanic run in 1960, the curtain fell and an era was over.

The only ship to maintain any semblance of transatlantic service today is the *QE2,* and she does it only as an incidental to her cruise-ship business. I made one voyage on her in 1971, going aboard in Southampton. She had been on a Mediterranean cruise and there was room for a few additional passengers between England and the U.S. It was not a happy trip. The first thing that struck me was that she had no deck space except on the boat deck, where the ship's forward motion guaranteed a gale of wind. All the transoceanic liners I had sailed on before provided wide promenade deck space, where the passengers could take their daily constitutionals. That walk was, in fact, one of the set pieces of the day. The food on the *QE2* was good, though not exceptional, but there was not the feeling of personal attention that had been so noticeable on the ships on regular runs.

Cruise *passengers* are different also. I am sure they are nice people, but all they seemed to be interested in was playing bridge or drinking. On the ships on a regular run the passengers were going somewhere, there was a purpose to the voyage. They had something to talk about. All cruise passengers discuss is what ports they have been to, where they are going on their next cruise, and where they have been on previous voyages. I found myself looking forward to our arrival in New York.

The saddest footnote to the character of the *QE2* came in an English newspaper I saw the other day. There was an advertisement coaxing the reader to take a two-day journey from Southampton to a couple of ports in France, returning to England within forty-eight hours. An adventure aptly called a booze cruise.

I suppose I feel sentimental about the ships that for so many years provided the umbilical cord between Europe and America because I am a sometime seaman, and have pounded my way across the North Atlantic to make a living. It is probably the toughest seafaring assignment in the world, and it is amazing that the finest maritime passenger service ever conceived should have been born of that unforgiving ocean. There were first-class passenger vessels plying other routes across the world (there are almost none anywhere now), but they could not compare with the leviathans of the Europe-America service. The world will never see their like again, but as long as anyone lives who sailed on them, their memory will stay ever green.

Shrinking Back to Size

Outside, the snow is piled so high in the window boxes that only the tips of the red-dyed ruscus we used for Christmas decorations are visible. The bay is gray and blotched with irregular ice floes that come and go with the tide. The birches and few maples in the lower woodlot resemble a Currier and Ives print; every branch and twig is etched sharp against the pewter of the water behind them. Western Mountain is black except where an occasional cut-over patch shows as a white handkerchief. It is a scene that would depress some, but one that I have come to love. It is part of the round of the seasons, and I know that, dreary as it may appear, it is only a phase, and a necessary one, in the turning of the wheel.

It has taken some time for me to learn that there is no beginning nor end, except for me, to the flow of time. When I was young I was always anticipating the future, giving up what I had then in anticipation of some future benediction. Now I am grown old, I am wiser. I enjoy each minute as it passes, perhaps because my own future no longer stretches ahead into a seeming infinity of years as it once did. I am more appreciative of the here and now. I survey little distances. I am microscopic rather than telescopic. Like the atomic scientist, I have discovered whole galaxies within a speck invisible to the naked eye.

I came home yesterday from a trip "up" to Boston. Someone, I think it was E. B. White, said that it is no good saying "up" to Boston unless you really felt you were going "up." When you are from "away," and that means from south or west of here, you feel when you leave Maine that you are going *down* to Boston. It takes a long time to adjust your compass. As seamen know, compass error is due to two influences. One is called deviation and the other variation. Deviation is caused by the ship's magnetism and can be compensated for, but variation depends upon where you are on the earth's surface, and constantly changes. I have been here long enough that my deviation is pretty well compensated, but variation still catches me out occasionally. I was all right yesterday, though. As those hundreds of ice-rimmed islands and frozen lakes slid by under the airplane I felt in my bones that I was headed *down* home. It was instinctive, not just an intellectual exercise. My internal compass never wavered.

I enjoyed my trip to the big city. I was with friends. I ate in some restaurants of a quality only to be found where there are many people. I went to the opera, a pleasure difficult to come by among all those ice-rimmed islands and frozen lakes. When we came out of the theater onto the snow-covered street my wife said to me, "How fresh this air feels!" I replied that it should, for what we had been breathing for the last three hours was not just second-hand air but about thousandth-hand. My enthusiasm for the advantages of city life was beginning to erode. There was too much of everything. There were too many people. Good people, I'm sure; kind people, earnest people, rich people, poor people—you name them, they were there. But there were too many of them. Everything was oversized. I found myself looking at the world through a wide-angle lens, and I wanted to get back to my microscope.

When I reclaimed my car at the airport in the Maine parking lot, the attendant looked at my three-day ticket and said, "Five dollars and fifteen cents, please," and added, "Did you have a good time in Boston?" I replied that I had, and how did he know I had been in Boston. He smiled and said, "It figures." As I drove away I pondered upon the neighborliness of small town and country people, and also did a fast bit of mental arithmetic and told myself that the parking tab in Boston would have been at least fifteen dollars instead of five.

When I drove into my dooryard I could hear Happy giving tongue in the kitchen. She can identify our car by its sound when it comes around the bend in the road. She was so glad to see us (after having felt she had been eternally deserted) that she had a little trouble with her plumbing. I walked over the brittle remains of the last snow to the barn, and fed a handful of grain to the bull while he batted his four-inch eyelashes at me. When I got back to the house, my wife had taken a couple of last summer's stuffed peppers out of the freezer and put them in the oven. While they were "hotting up," I mixed a martini that I figured cost twenty-five cents, against the two-fifty I had paid in Boston. Everything was shrinking back to size again.

Matters of the Spirit

Nor stony tower, nor walls of beaten brass.
Nor airless dungeon, nor strong links of iron,
Can be retentive to the strength of spirit.

— Shakespeare, *Julius Caesar,* Act I, scene iii

White Space

I read in a morning paper recently a prediction that by the year 2000 privacy as we have known it will no longer be possible. Even allowing for the natural pessimism of prophets, this is a disquieting thought. For me, most frightening is the realization that with each succeeding generation the *desire* for privacy, for solitude, is exhibited by fewer people.

My own pessimism is not due solely to having had five or six grandchildren or great grandchildren underfoot all summer, but the fact is that, someone having primed the pump, my mind has been busy selecting from its accumulation of experiences facts to support the idea, and has been only too successful in finding them.

When I read a book or listen to a thesis my first reaction is agreement; it is not until some time later that a suspicion begins to stir within me that there is something to be said on the other side of the picture. I suppose this proves, if it proves anything, that I am of an agreeable disposition and unlikely to seek out controversy. But I think it also indicates that I, and others like me, are Solitaries, as they used to call some of the old monks. We need time and privacy to arrive at conclusions. I am not suggesting that people of this temperament are superior to those who love nothing better than a good dispute and seldom really listen to their opponents, being too interested in what they themselves are going to say next. What I am suggesting, even though to me it seems sad, is that in an overcrowded world with no privacy, the people of a combative and opinionated nature are going to be the ones who survive, though I like to think there will be somewhere a place and a service to be performed by those of a more reflective disposition.

I do not believe that very much original thinking gets done within the confines of a political convention or the walls of a crowded lecture hall, even though there are many people who are never happier than when in such an atmosphere. Henry Thoreau once remarked that he needed a wide margin to his life, and by inference that all men do—what the advertising trade calls white space. Newton came upon the law of gravity under an apple tree; Malthus, his doctrine of population control while walking the long, lonely roads of Scandinavia; Darwin, the theory of evolution when he was living in the quiet English countryside after returning from the voyage of the *Beagle*.

Gardening is more than growing plants. It is a solitary, contemplative person's occupation, giving opportunity for thought in an increasingly thoughtless world. Philosophers are out of fashion; this is the day of the engineer, the scientist, and the politician. The first two are so successful in their creation of material blessings that the latter is unable to distribute them equitably. The genie is out of the bottle, and we can neither get him back in nor control him. We need a few more Thoreaus or Pascals.

I have been writing this in my little summerhouse; its casement windows are open to the sunshine, and my dog is pulling burrs out of her coat at my feet. The great golden trumpets of a hybrid lily are swaying gently in a light breeze, and beyond them half a dozen cedar waxwings are rifling a honeysuckle bush of its scarlet berries.

A garden is a fine place to retreat from the frustrations and insanities of the twentieth century. Don't misunderstand me. It offers no freely given panacea. You get out of it what you put into it, both flowers and contentment. It does not always come out nice and even at the end, as man, being the arithmetical animal that he is, would like to have it. A garden is like real life, not like a novel. You cannot take a look at the last page to see what the end is going to be. Sometimes there is not any end, except for you. Life and the garden go on.

A Walk-On Part

Most of the nonstop chit-chat that goes on between people in close daily communication has no significance. We talk not because we have something to say, but because we have an abhorrence of silence. If a minute or so elapses without remark, we begin to fidget and feel embarrassed. I don't know how it is now, but when I used to visit England regularly I was struck by the fact that there was complete silence at the end of their radio broadcasts, sometimes for several minutes, before the next program began. I don't know if this means the English are less talkative or just that they use a different system, but an American listener would immediately assume there were technical difficulties and twist the dial—or kick the machine.

William Penn the Proprietor (or William Penn his father, I'm not sure which) said, "True silence . . . is a great virtue; it covers folly, keeps secrets, avoids disputes and prevents sin." The Bible concurs: "No one is sooner taken for a wise man than the fool who keeps his mouth shut." Think how much folly would be covered, secrets kept, disputes avoided, and sin escaped if politicians, for example, were stricken dumb. If each candidate were required to prepare a written position paper of not more than a thousand words, setting forth exactly what he proposed to do if elected, and rest his case there, how quiet our airwaves would be. Of course, that would not give much margin in which to castigate an opponent, but you can get a lot of meat into a thousand words. That's something writers learn. A two thousand-word draft is usually improved if cut in half. Richard Mitchell, writing in "Less Than Words Can Say," remarks that "the mind is a rudderless wanderer," and that when we sit down to think what we are usually doing is letting it drift.

Old Ben Franklin understood man's weakness for words when he wrote, "None preaches better than the ant and she says nothing." I guess that's a good reason for keeping the tongue between the teeth. Or maybe it's best to take a cue from country people, who have learned to talk to themselves (sometimes out loud), to the amusement of the uninitiated. For the most part these country people have discovered that they are their own most interesting company.

It may be fair to say that country people talk to themselves because there is no one else to talk to in the wide open spaces they inhabit. But many people choose rural living to find just that solitude. Not absolute solitude like that of Robinson Crusoe, but the sort that the eighteenth-century poet William Cowper had in mind when he wrote, "How sweet, how passing sweet is solitude! / But grant me still a friend in my retreat, / Whom I may whisper, solitude is sweet."

My farm in Pennsylvania, halfway between Philadelphia and Baltimore (not properly a farm, as it was only fifteen acres and my sole crop was a field of corn), was surrounded by real dairy farms and a scattering of mushroom houses. My nearest neighbor's dwelling and barn were on the other side of a valley a half mile away, and in the farther distance in other directions I could see green fields and more barns and houses. Just over the crest of a small hill to the north, a raveling of smoke rose on chilly mornings. The house it came from was not visible, but if I walked to the high spot at the end of my farm road, I could just glimpse a chimney pot.

People who visited me at Serendipity—for that was what I called the place—asked the same question I get here: Am I not lonesome living out of earshot of neighbors? The answer was, as it still is, that while I enjoy a few friends and an occasional visitor, I am not discontented with such solitude as I have—which is not all that much. I have never been lonely.

Sharing is the essential bond in all happy human relationships, even if all there is to be shared is solitude. I am fond of a good measure of it—more of it, I suspect, than most people—but after a few hours alone in the garden, I am happy to come in and drink a cup of coffee with my wife and report to her on the state of the snap peas or the depredations of the deer. Some might say that weeding a garden, or sailing a boat single-handed, if you like, is not really solitude, because you have the companionship of your occupation. Fair enough. Certainly busy solitude is the only pregnant kind, the only kind that gives birth to anything. Sitting on a flagpole is solitary, and so is walking alone and friendless on the streets of a big city. But it is not the sort of solitude that induces creative thinking. It does not make the mind stronger and turn it inward to learn about itself.

Constant contact with other people is debilitating. One is subjected to a barrage of opinions, few of consequence. When I am weeding my carrots, they do not talk back to me. My mind can wander happily, like the ball in a pinball machine, along whatever tangent the previous thought may have directed it. There is constant interest in where the ball will go next, where the last thought will lead the next one. Many people do not like to think, or may not choose to use the thinking equipment they have, but if one does, it is a fascinating occupation. It is inexpensive, and much more rewarding than cuddling a can of beer and watching a parcel of overpaid and overmuscled gladiators beating on each other on the television.

Somebody once said of thinking that if a political leader could make the voters believe they were thinking, they would keep reelecting him until he died, but if he really made them think, they'd run him out of office. Thinking is a dangerous pastime (see what happened to Socrates and Jesus), but it is the root of all good just as it is the root of all evil. Maybe that is why it is best done alone.

A safe place is your garden. Pascal, whose *Pensées* I recommend, said that man was lost and saved in a garden. Meaning, of course, the Garden of Eden and the Garden of Gethsemane. Whether you get lost or saved is up to you. Most of us pursue our journey across life's stage as walk-on characters and have no lines. Making the part meaningful makes all the difference.

On the Seventh Day We Rest

If you live in a city apartment, or a condominium in the suburbs, or even a so-called townhouse in the country (I have seen these last in the most un-urban surroundings), you don't have to do more than get your clothing out of storage to prepare for winter. In the city, you spend less time in the open. You can go from heated house to heated store or office in a heated car or subway or bus, and exposure to the elements in minimal. Winter is just a nuisance. Snow gets dirty even as it falls, and it messes up the sidewalks, particularly at street corners. A couple of inches create the most horrendous traffic jam; six or eight bring "civilization" to a stumbling halt.

Because there is less to do to prepare for winter, its warnings go unnoticed. Mornings are a little colder. Street lights, activated by an automatic switch, go on a little earlier. The Academy of Music and the Opera House advertise the start of their winter seasons. The stores begin to advertise Christmas sometime in October, leapfrogging Thanksgiving altogether, and the travel agencies burst forth with colorful posters telling of the blue skies and coral beaches of Bermuda, Florida, and the romantic Caribbean.

Everybody in town knows that winter is something they don't like—everybody except the young, who whiz through the country on superhighways en route to ski slopes. *They* really don't see much of winter either. They get from the turnpike, which is the same winter or summer, over the shortest side road they can find to Slippery Mountain Ski Lodge, where they spend the daylight hours being hauled to the top of the mountain so they can slide to the bottom. In the evenings they gather with all the other city folk for an *aprés ski* in front of a blazing hearth with a hot buttered rum. They do the same thing they do in town—crowd as many people as possible into as small a space as possible. They are uncomfortable outside, perhaps even find it a little scary, when it gets dark. They prefer to be where there are others to rub elbows with. If it doesn't snow at the proper time, the entrepreneurs of the ski slopes play God and manufacture their own white stuff. Off the highways and the ski slopes, the customers are as out of place as a nightclub singer in a lobster joint.

In the real countryside, where people live and work, by early November there are signs of approaching winter. The first warning comes with the departure of tourists. Soon after, the larger restaurants and motels close, because there is not enough business to keep them going. They cater to the elbow-to-elbow crowd. Smaller places hang on for a while, but by and by even they put up their shutters. Then, with the summer houses boarded up and chains swinging across driveways, comes the lull before real winter.

The leaves have been gone from the trees for several weeks, and at first the roads seem strange because the woodland is so bright. Places and views long forgotten suddenly appear again. Coming down a road, you turn a corner—and ahead are miles of open water glinting through the bare branches. Where a couple of weeks ago you looked at what appeared to be dense woodland stretching all the way to Canada, now you see a house or an open field.

With the leaves swept by nature's broom into tidy windrows behind the rocks and hedges, you become aware that your provident neighbors have accumulated reassuring woodpiles not too far from their kitchen doors. Where you can see into the barns, you glimpse split stove lengths stacked neatly against the cold to come. Many countrymen's houses have always been heated with wood, and while there has been a drift toward the convenience of oil during the last few decades, wood never has been wholly banished. Many houses heated by oil still have accommodations for wood stoves that are moved in from the barn during the winter. Even more country dwellers never gave up their wood (or wood-and-gas) ranges, because there is nothing cozier or better to cook on than a wood range.

Another sure indication of cold ahead is the pile of spruce or balsam fir boughs in dooryards along the way. Some of the greenery is for banking against the house foundations to catch the snow and insulate the basement, while the rest is for wreathing. Snow is the very best insulation ever created. If eight or ten inches of snow falls immediately before hard cold sets in, the ground beneath it will go through the whole winter with little or no frozen soil. When snow lodges for the winter on brush around the cellar wall, all inside is snug. A lot of householders in these modern times tack plastic or tarpaper on the lower course of clapboards or shingles and cover the bottom edge with soil. We do both, use tarpaper and cover it with spruce boughs. It is so windproof that I have to cut out a small section over one of the cellar windows so fresh air can get into my cold cellar, where apples and potatoes and home-canned vegetables and pickles and jams and other luscious oddments from the garden live.

The rest of the greenery in my neighbors' dooryards is used to make basic undecorated wreaths. Most buyers stipulate that the brush not be cut before November 5, and that it and the wreaths be stacked outdoors in a cool, moist place. Wreathing is a big business here between November and Christmas. Apart from the holiday money it provides, wreathing is as traditional to Maine as digging clams. It is a sure sign of approaching winter, for good wreathers like a frost or two before cutting the brush: they say it makes the spills (needles) stick on better. The wreaths not only leave the state, piled perilously high on trucks headed south, but they decorate Maine houses from early December to Easter—not just a meager wreath on the front door, but often one in each window, several on the side of a house, or welcoming the mailman to postboxes gay with greens and ribbons.

I once saw in a national newspaper a communication from an enthusiastic conservationist, asking the public to "Vote for ecology by buying artificial Christmas trees." I do not quite know how you can vote for ecology, which is going to be here, vote or no vote, but I suppose the writer meant vote to conserve our natural resources. Christmas trees, however, are a crop, like cabbages. The cutting and sale of Christmas trees and the making of wreaths contribute in no small measure to our economy, and families would have to cut back on their Christmas festivities if they were denied this source of income. I think maybe the letter writer was a Californian, someone who had no knowledge of local conditions and to whom Maine was a foreign country three thousand miles away. Here evergreens regenerate and grow with enthusiasm wherever land is opened in the woods. The seeds have been waiting for a chance to germinate, and removing the shade and exposing the soil gives them the opportunity. We are, in fact, faced with an embarrassment of riches, as they grow so closely that most of them die in the fierce competition for light. They should be thinned to become well-branched Christmas trees, and these in turn can be cut, leaving space for those remaining to make pulpwood in another thirty or forty years, when the cycle starts over. These small volunteers are so prolific along the roadside that they are sprayed by the utility companies and mowed down by the road crews, so a load of Christmas trees lurching along the uneven country roads on the first leg of their trip to the cities doesn't bother me at all; I just see Maine's economy on the move and winter coming one step closer.

I guess there are not many people living in the city who take down screens, wash windows, and put up storm sash and storm doors to ward off the winter winds. You can't do it in an apartment house, and the modern townhouses and condominiums either have the whole business built in, use thermopane, or are hermetically sealed summer and winter so that one just flips the switch to change the season.

Here, we clean up the debris, put brush on the flower borders and seaweed on the asparagus bed, pick the last odd flowers and blueberries, place netting over the prize shrubs so the deer won't browse them—and, as the Lord did, on the seventh day, we rest.

A Sometime Thing

There is a lot of talk these days about limited nuclear war. Such idiocy! We can no more have limited nuclear war than we can have limited death. You live, or you die. The *world* will not be destroyed by nuclear war. The world has been here for uncountable eons, and will continue—and so will some of the human race. What will be destroyed is the civilization we have so laboriously erected over the last few millenia. I do not say that an even greater one may not someday, down the long corridors of future time, succeed it, but all we have known and cherished will be gone. All that will be left when the dust has settled will be man's indestructable spirit, which will still wonder at the spring and the autumn; at skies filled with misty clouds, ragged and formless, against a pale, forget-me-not blue background.

Every winter, after months of cold and snow, I wait for the Ides of March with the same feeling that primitive man must have had: that winter has been conquered and better days are ahead, even if the air is still cold and the temperature barely above freezing. Each spring there comes this time of awakening. I have it now, and my diary says I had it forty years ago. Turning back, I found: "I have been in the garden almost the whole day. A buffeting, blustering wind out of the west pressed against my body with a personal roughness, as though there was a conflict to be determined between us. Great dark shadows alternated with intervals of brilliant sunshine and the air was clean and brittle, as though it washed over me pure and untainted from another world, the world of that immensity of blue space beyond the farthest star. I was happier than I have been in weeks."

I can look forward only to single years now and no longer count on decades, but my reactions are no different. When I am where the gale can assail me, I make sure my next point of refuge is not too far off. The wind's strength is the same, but mine is not. The breeze has still the same wine-clear quality—coming high out of the northwest, swooping down over the spruces that surround my hayfield, struggling with the cedars protecting my garden, and, once over that obstacle, tearing my hat from my head and chasing off down the hill to lift the spume from the whitecaps with which it paints the dark waters of the bay.

We speak of change, but there is no change. Not in the brief span of the human race. I can hear Virgil's voice, two thousand years gone, singing of his old Corycian swain, who "when sullen winter was still bursting rocks with the cold . . . [was] chiding laggard summer and the loitering zephyrs," even as I do today.

Long before Virgil another poet sang, in the Song of Solomon, "Arise, my love, my fair one, and come away: for lo, the winter is passed, the rain is over and gone. The flowers appear on the earth and the time of singing of birds has come."

Earlier still, in the dawn of our history, when man had not long passed that divide between the unconscious animal and the state where he was capable of reflection upon his own actions, he must have waited apprehensively for spring just as we do, and rejoiced when, despite his gravest forebodings, soft winds melted the ice and snow and the grass turned green once again and the trees unfolded their leaves.

Spring in Maine is like that woman in *Porgy and Bess,* a sometime thing. One day she blows hot and the next, cold. Some day there will come a warm rain and sunshine to follow, and in the twinkling of an eye all of spring will arrive and be just as quickly gone—as fast as we shall be raised from the dead at the last trump, according to Corinthians.

We get our notions of spring from the poets, most of whom were English and thus accustomed to a spring that began in late February (when we in Maine are still under three feet of snow) and lasted until June (when in much of America you can fry an egg on the sidewalk).

Swinburne sings: "For winter's rains and ruins are over / and in green underwood and cover blossom by blossom the spring begins." And Coleridge writes, "And the spring comes slowly up this way." In Maine it's more like Henry Van Dyke's, "The first day of spring is one thing, and the first spring day is another. The difference between them is sometimes as great as a month." This business of spring coming "blossom by blossom," or "slowly up this way," just proves that you can't transport seasons from one country to another.

I love spring, but I would love her more were she not so impetuous when she finally reaches me. She embraces me with such a multitude of beauties, such overwhelming affection, such passion and heat, that I am left trembling—and, if truth be known, a little frightened. I know what I have to do, but I have neither the time nor the stamina to accomplish it.

One day the wind will caress me and my garden, and overnight daffodils and tulips will burst into flower, the shadbush will clothe the countryside in pink and white gossamer, the apple trees will shake down clouds of petals (those the waxwings have not eaten), lilies will push up little molehills as they emerge from their winter rest, and the clematis will extend its waving shoots a foot a night. For the vegetable gardener, rhubarb and asparagus will grow faster than they can be picked, and the peas, planted in the mud a month back, will push up their little croziers and reach for something to climb on.

Bobolinks, which arrive with the asparagus, sing their hearts out from dawn to dark, their song so liquid and unrehearsed it sounds like water pouring over rocks in a little brook. The barn swallows take up residency early each spring and engage in aerial acrobatics, picking up the odd blackfly, the curse of May in Maine, and before you know it you're searching for that day that is so rare in June. The sky will be a shade bluer than the bluets that grow by the millions in all the damp spots in the meadows. Not the tiniest cotton puff of a cloud will mar the heavens, and the last blizzard is a forgotten memory.

In the spring the new foliage of the blueberries shows in irregular patches, here pale green, there shades of pink, for the leaves of variant forms differ in color as do those of the shadbush. The areas still exhibiting the annual fall "burn" vary from black to cinnamon. Blueberry barrens are interesting. Many of them here show rifts of ledge breaking through the thin soil, and are studded with rocks left over from the last ice age. The enormous boulders remind one of megalithic monuments—our own Stonehenge. The barrens are haunted by birds; on one spring day, as I sat waiting while my wife was visiting down the street, I spotted a dove, some robins, a flycatcher, goldfinches, and others I couldn't identify. A small hawk, possibly a sparrow hawk, perched on a great boulder, periodically swooping off in graceful curves to hang fluttering in the air (looking, I suppose, for some victim) before returning to his perch. It seemed totally unconcerned by me, although I was no more than ten feet away.

Attempts have been made to harvest blueberries mechanically with some success, but raking in fields like these is, and will remain, a job for human hands. No machine could cope with this lunar landscape. So much of our life has come under the control of the machine that it is unusual to find an area modern technology cannot invade. Searing blueberry fields by kerosene burners has become commonplace, but in the wild areas, old methods prevail. In the fall, the fields are strewn heavily with hay and fired, pruning the blueberries and killing weed seeds as the line of little flames and smoke creeps across the open fields. It may be less efficient than an oil burn but it is more picturesque, and the material to accomplish it is near at hand in the old run-out pastures.

When I went to pick up Helen, I told her it was far too nice a day to go home, so she said, "Let's go to the Bagaduce Lunch and eat a hot dog and watch the tidal rapids." We did. As a concession to *haut cuisine,* I stopped at Merrill & Hinckeley's and bought a bottle of wine and a couple of plastic glasses. (I always keep a corkscrew in the car with the other first aid equipment.) As we sat behind a spruce tree out of the wind, watching the blankets of foam from the falls blow onto the bank, a young couple arrived in an ancient Jaguar. As they stumbled down the steep, rough bank, balancing plates of hamburgers, the boy turned to me and asked in an aggrieved tone, "Do you believe $3.25 for a dish of fried clams? Wow! How long has that been?" I looked at his New York license plate and thought, *spring has sprung, the tourist season has now begun.* And today, nothing has really changed—except the prices!

Command

Wars are fought by young men, and there has never yet been a war when those who returned were not restless and uncertain about the perils of peace. You can imagine Roman soldiers returning from the Punic wars wondering what they would do back among the civilians in Rome, or legionnaires who were recalled from Britain in 407 A.D. (where they had been fighting a guerilla war against the Picts and the Scots) looking for jobs and finally joining somebody else's army to fight somebody else's war.

When I came back from my war I was similarly restless, and as there were no other wars going on at the moment except for an internal fracas in Russia (which I looked in on and found uninteresting), I wandered off to sea. I had no idea of making seafaring a profession, but the sea, like the juice of the poppy, is addictive. Had it not been for a woman (women also being addictive) and a special occurrence, the details of which are too involved to describe here, I would still be calling myself a sailor. I never managed, though, to get the salt out of my blood.

I was a seaman for ten years in my youth. It becomes a smaller portion of my life as time goes by, but those were impressionable years, and the sea left an indelible mark. It is difficult for modern Americans to appreciate the influence the seafaring profession has upon a man. A hundred years ago they would have understood—at least, those who lived along the eastern seaboard would—for America was then a seafaring nation. In addition to the clipper ships that we are still so proud of (though there were relatively few of them), there were hundreds—nay, thousands—of humbler craft, both sail and steam, laboring along the coast and on deeper waters every hour of every day of the year. Now there are almost no coastal vessels and but a modest number of deepwater ships flying the American flag. Most people have little contact with seamen, and, if they think of them at all, carry in their minds fictional characters such as O'Neill's Hairy Ape.

Even with all the modern equipment making it possible for ships to be in constant communication with the land, there remains a vast and unbridgeable chasm between the demands made on a seaman by his profession and those required of a landsman. The sea is unforgiving of the slightest carelessness or neglect or inattention, and that fact molds a seaman's character. The minute he sets in motion the power below decks that causes the first hesitant trembling of the hull, he is in a different world. He does not have a profession, he *is* the profession. He never closes his desk and goes home, because his ship is his his home. The final decision is always his, as is the ultimate blame if anything goes wrong.

Along the New England coast there are many competent small-boat sailors. I do not belittle their skill, but sailing for pleasure—going to sea or remaining ashore as they choose, and hauling their vessels out for the winter—bears no resemblance to the life and obligations faced by a working seaman. The only profession that bears any comparison is that of a commercial airplane pilot. Danger faces him also if he is even momentarily inattentive, careless, or casual about his job, but his responsibility continues for only hours, not weeks.

One day more than fifty years ago, I stepped from a hot and dusty street in San Pedro, California into a wooden building displaying a small sign at sidewalk level proclaiming it to be the local headquarters of the United States Steamboat Inspection Service. San Pedro was not much of a place in those days, but it was hoped it would eventually be the port of Los Angeles. There were a few docks and warehouses, sheltered by a long stone breakwater constructed to protect a harbor that would not otherwise have had much to recommend it. San Pedro boasted only a few houses, and about the only entertainment was that offered by a movie theater, a couple of establishments of ill repute, and the opportunity of fishing off the breakwater.

I was there because the S.S. *City of Honolulu,* on which I had served as helmsman, had been destroyed by fire, on its maiden voyage, halfway between Los Angeles and Honolulu. The crew and passengers survived and in due course were taken to Los Angeles. After several weeks the company secured a substitute ship, and the Master, who had taken a fancy to me during the fire, said I could have the job of fourth officer if I could get my license. My visit to the Steamboat Inspection Office was so I might take the required examination. Three days later, I walked out with a document certifying that I was competent to serve as third mate on "any vessel of any tonnage on any ocean."

The ship I was to sail on was named the *Calawaii.* She was a smallish, but very comfortable, passenger vessel with some cargo space. Her owners, the Los Angeles Steamship Company, had brought her secondhand, refitted her, painted her white to give her a tropical appearance, and rushed her into service.

I can still remember, after all these years, the first time I stepped on her bridge as a watch officer. Being the junior mate I had the eight to midnight watch, and when the time came for me to go on duty, I was as apprehensive as if I had never before set foot on a ship. We sailed at noon and by eight that evening were well offshore, headed into a long Pacific swell. The sea was calm, but as I ran up the companionway to the bridge, the vessel rose to meet me, pressing against my feet and then falling away as the swell rolled under her. I left below me the chatter of our passengers and the lights and music in the saloon and stepped onto the bridge, into a different world. The only sounds there were the whine of the wind in the rigging, the steady throb of the engines, and the creaking of the bulkheads of the pilot house. It was fifteen minutes before the hour, and the mate seemed surprised to see me so early, but he said nothing beyond "Good evening, Mister."

I had rehearsed a hundred times what I was going to do on my first watch, so after acknowledging his greeting I stepped into the chart-room, where a low light under a blue shade shone on the chart and the night-order book. I read the orders and signed the book and carefully, as though I were Magellan beating through the Straits, checked the course and distance run. As I walked through the pilot-house to the bridge, the helmsman behind the wheel, legs spread, and swaying gently with the ship's motion, looked up. The only light came from the binnacle, and it gave his face a saturnine aspect.

Outside, the mate was leaning against the rail with his chin on the weathercloth—the "dodger" that serves to deflect the constant wind created by a ship under way. He gave me the course and speed and remarked that the Old Man had told him he would be up about four bells and that if I needed him before then I should give a toot on the whistle, but said nothing else. A minute or so later the relieving helmsman appeared; he gave me the reading of the log and took over the wheel.

For the first time in my life, I was alone in command of a ship. I felt detached from reality. There was a half moon sliding along between broken clouds, and patches of thin fog. When I walked out to the wing of the bridge and looked forward, a phosphorescent plume broke away from the waves under the forefoot and hissed alongside beneath me. Astern, the wake boiled and swirled under the counter, fading into a faint line in the far distance. I was enchanted. I stood there for a long time, quite motionless, until the helmsman struck one bell and was answered by the lookout repeating it from the crow's nest. Then he added the timeless words called out by lookouts over the centuries: "Lights are burning bright, sir." Though I subsequently stood many watches on many ships, in good weather and bad, in many parts of the world, I shall never forget that first experience.

Behind today's men who "go down to the sea in ships" stretches a line reaching back into a past so remote as to be beyond historical recall. The skills developed by the Phoenicians—and even the terms of their marine insurance contracts dating from eight hundred years before Christ, when their ships sailed from Tyre and Sidon to trade in the Mediterranean—are still in use as part of seafaring knowledge, and the Phoenicians were relatively recent members of the craft. It is the weight of this past, and the fact that despite modern technologies the final showdown is between man and the sea, that make seamen a different breed. Once saltwater is in the blood it can never be entirely removed.

I suppose that is why I bought my house by the sea. When the wind is in the right direction, southeast, I can hear the bell buoy tolling out beyond Hog Island. I can watch the gulls, replicas of those that trailed behind my ships on the other side of the world, buffet the updrafts that rise along the shoreline to sail, wing high, wing low, over my house, which stands silently facing out to sea, as it has done for more than one hundred years.

To Be a Gentleman

If asked the significance of the word "gentleman," many people today would respond that it indicates the entrance to a men's lavatory—a sad comedown for a word that began as a designation for "a man of gentle birth, one entitled to bear arms, though not noble, but applied to any person of distinction."

As the years have passed, there have been other definitions, such as "a man of superior position in society" and "a man of money and leisure." In the Edwardian period the word, by general agreement, was taken to mean a man who was generous, courteous, polite, and of chivalrous instincts and fine feelings, a person upon whose word one could depend and whose honesty went beyond the technicalities. Thoreau put it crisply, as he had the ability to do, when he said of Cyrus Hubbard that he was a man "of a certain New England probity and worth, immortal and natural, like a natural product, like the sweetness of a nut, like the toughness of hickory," and that it was "a great encouragement that an honest man makes this world his abode. . . . The farmer spoke to me . . . clean, cold, moderate as the snow. He does not melt the snow where he treads." In other words, a gentleman.

I think it says something of the society in which we live that we do not have in everyday usage today a word with the significance of the word "gentleman." It is something to regret. Of course, there are still gentlemen in the world—but not, I think, as many; and certainly the model of an old-fashioned gentleman is not held up as an example toward which to strive. Today a man should be "macho" and, if in business, "make" a lot of money. Being financially successful is the most important goal. Even our universities, which should suggest that the enduring and worthwhile thing in life is character, instead tell students that if they obtain a bachelor's degree, a master's degree—or, at the pinnacle, a doctorate—they will accumulate more money. And the schools offer statistics to prove it.

There is nothing wrong with being successful financially, but the possession of money does not necessarily make a man a gentleman—nor does the lack of it make it more difficult to be one. I do believe, though, that being a gentleman is more important than being rich.

When I use the word *gentleman,* of course I am not unaware of the same qualities inherent in the term *lady.* The commonly understood meaning of lady also has suffered a decline. One of the finest ladies it has been my privilege to know lived in this village. She is dead now, having finally paid her debt to mortality at an advanced age. When I compare her with the "ladies" who figure so frequently in the public press, I wonder where our society is headed. Millie once said to me: "Mr. Barrette, I don't understand about senators and congressmen having to draw up a written code of ethics. Goodness gracious, you *know* whether something is right or wrong. You just know! Anyway, if you have to have it in print—it is all in the Bible." Of course, not so many people read the Bible nowadays. The Supreme Court, in its wisdom, has prohibited it from being read in school, so you can't blame that on the educators.

Millie's comment that "You just know!" says it all. My grandparents, who looked after me, knew their Bible, as did most everyone in those days. They knew it in the same way they knew Shakespeare, on an intellectual level. They did not invoke the name of the Lord very often. Grandfather would say "God damn it!" in times of stress, but he was careful not to do it in the presence of women. In one way, though, my grandparents were very like Millie. They believed there were some things that one "just knew."

Grandmother taught by example, but it was left to grandfather, as head of the household, to be specific. I can still remember, after all these years, his telling me that there were some things a gentleman didn't do. You just didn't do them. They were not very big things, but large things do grow out of small ones. He told me that one never stared at people who were disfigured or in any way handicapped, because to do so would embarrass them. That did not mean they should be ignored, merely that care should be taken to respect their special feelings. One never raised one's voice or lost one's temper, he said, because to do so was vulgar. One didn't lie, but on the other hand one didn't tell the truth either if the truth would cause pain to another. You must always be particularly careful in your dealings with those of a lesser station in life, my Victorian grandfather stressed, and you were, without saying, scrupulously honest, to the penny. He also taught me that a gentleman never kissed and told, counsel that seems to be more honored in the breach now than in the observance. There was much more, but it was of the same pattern. Propriety, simplicity, and thoughtfulness come as close as can be said in a few words. My grandfather agreed with Thackeray: "To be a gentleman is to be honest, to be gentle, to be generous, to be brave, to be wise, and possessing all those qualities to exercise them in the most graceful manner."

Maybe it's too simplistic to suggest that adherence to these principles might solve many of the problems facing our confused and unhappy world today—but it wouldn't hurt to try.

Benign Neglect

We have in our church a young matron named Penelope (I mention the name because it is old-fashioned and charms me) who has two small females in the three-to-four-year-old range who tag along with her like Mary's little lambs. They are quite unselfconscious and charming, and the reason is, I think, that their mother treats them with benign neglect. When one stands on the edge of a chair and is in imminent danger of a tumble, Penelope does not, as most people would do, either grab her or yell, "Hey, look out!" but merely smiles and looks the other way. Kids being as indestructible as golf balls anyway, no mortal injury has ever occurred.

I am moved to this dissertation on child care because of an article I read in an English magazine. It was written by Ian Niall and called "Journeys in the Dark," and as it was set in the English countryside where I grew up, it stirred recollections in my mind. Niall speaks of riding along narrow country lanes in a trap behind a pony and how little one could see on dark nights. He speaks too of the gig's lamps being lighted by candles. I remember them; they merely made the darkness more visible.

I can't remember much about my early life in America because I left when I was less than five years old, but I do recall that I was afraid of the dark. After I was put to bed, I hid my head under the covers so I would not hear the branches of a tree scratching against the house, or the shutters rattling on windy nights. The place where I lived was (or so it seemed to me) deep in the woods, where all sorts of spooky things wandered. I am sure the very old lady with whom I lived took good care of me, but in those far-off days even small children, or most of them anyway, lived according to rules, and when I was put to bed, the door was closed and I was to be heard from no more until morning.

With my maternal grandparents in England my life was very different, because *they* were very different. I lived with them instead of with my parents because my father was a mining engineer whose profession kept him traveling around the world all his life, and my mother went with him.

My English grandmother was called "little Granny" because she was diminutive, under five feet, whereas my American grandmother was known as "big Granny" because she was a foot taller. Little Granny or my grandfather would put me to bed on time as had always been done, but when I ventured to ask them if the door might be left open a crack, it was left open a *wide* crack. I did not have to duck my head under the covers any more, and I enjoyed seeing the shadowy light and hearing the murmur of conversation from downstairs. One night I crept out of my bed and sat on the top step, listening. I am sure I had no idea of what the talk was about, but it was fascinating. Of course I got caught, but nothing drastic happened. I guess I was just put back to bed with the door still open.

When I became a little older I was allowed to stay up later. The living room had a fireplace that was flanked on one side by bookcases and on the other by a sort of built-in chest with a cushioned seat on top. I was allowed to curl up with a book amidst the cushions, and, as with Penelope's children, no one took much notice of me. As I could read quite well by the time I was six, and the house was filled with books, I soon learned to live my own life, and I suppose I was not much of a bother. What happened most nights was that I went to sleep on the chest and sooner or later someone lugged me up to bed.

In those long gone days there were no radios or television sets. Also, where I lived there was no electricity, so the rooms were lighted with oil lamps. The dining room had a fancy chandelier that let down from the ceiling to be filled and cleaned, but the room where we sat most of the time in the evening had several lamps scattered around on various tables. Although I am sure that whoever had to tend the lamps did not miss cleaning the chimneys with newspaper and filling the containers with oil after electric lights took over, there is a certain quality to lamplight that is missing from more convenient modern lighting. There is something else, too: even carefully trimmed oil lamps burn with a slight flicker and give off considerable heat. Perhaps that is why I always fell asleep in my chimney corner, and why grandfather, after a good dinner and a glass of port and a cigar and the London *Times,* would soon say, "Well, Mother, we have to be up early in the morning. Don't you think we had better go to bed?" I don't know why he had to get up early. He arose at 6:45 every morning anyway, and made sure I did the same.

I can't remember either of them worrying much about me. I recall falling in the pond one day and coming home covered with mud; not being able to think up any good excuse, I attempted to divert their attention by asking if they knew what tadpoles smelled like—and if they did not, they could smell me. I can't remember what happened, but I am sure not very much. I guess they worked on Penelope's theory that the best way to raise children is to let them do it themselves.

My Neighbor, Andy White

[Author's note: This piece was writen eight years before E.B. White's death on October 1, 1985. His passing left our village a poorer place.]

When I was asked to review *The Essays of E.B. White* and extend my remarks into a consideration of the author's life, I had some hesitation about accepting the assignment.

It is true that I have lived in the same village with E.B. White for twenty-five years, and in a small rural community there are few secrets. It is true also that we are casual friends, exchanging greetings at the post office or village store and on occasion discussing chicks (feathered) over a martini, but I did not think that degree of intimacy endowed me with much insight about the workings of his mind. Although I would have had no reluctance about making guesses concerning some other writer whose work interested me but with whom I was unacquainted personally, I felt constrained where my neighbor was concerned, for fear of overstepping the bounds of friendship. When I voiced these concerns, I was told, "The man is, of course, a famous figure . . . I should think that a low-key piece written in your normal gentlemanly manner could not possible be offensive or exploitative. Anyway . . . it occurs to me that he cannot lay much of a claim to absolute privacy in view of the book of his personal letters he has just published."

The argument was persuasive. Whether what I have to say will be any addition to the lore about America's greatest essayist is, however, debatable, because so much already has been written. The only thing I can guarantee is that it will be prejudiced, as I have an affection for the man and an admiration for his writing.

The dust jacket comment on *The Essays of E.B. White* says that he has published nineteen books. I own and have read fifteen. The *Essays,* I hope, is not his last. It contains various oddments purloined from earlier volumes, plus "a number of pieces that are appearing for this first time between covers." Only three essays—"The World of Tomorrow," "On a Florida Key," and "Once More to the Lake"—are extracted from my favorite book, *One Man's Meat,* the first of his collections of essays.

While E.B. White had published several volumes prior to the appearance of *One Man's Meat* in 1942 (among them *Every Day Is Saturday,* a collection of short paragraphs from the New Yorker that flickered like summer lightning as a suggestion of what might be ahead), it was not until *One Man's Meat* was published that his now characteristic style really became apparent. As he says himself, "There are as many kinds of essays as there are human attitudes or poses, as many flavors as there are Howard Johnson ice creams." But running through all of E.B. White's writings is his own special style, like a B-positive blood type. It does not make much difference whether he is writing about sulfur water in the kitchen sink in his Florida cottage or the diet of a seagull in Maine—his individual touch shows through. Almost everyone who has reviewed his books or analyzed his writing has offered an interpretation, but I doubt that anything as elusive as one human being's way of looking at life actually can be nailed down.

About as near as I can come to an explanation is to say that he has an ability to arrange ordinary simple words in such a fashion that magic happens. Not many writers have it. Shakespeare had it to perfection. I never have been able to explain why "In sooth I know not why I am so sad," the opening line of *The Merchant of Venice,* continues to hold me after fifty or sixty years of reading. There have, of course, been other writers with this gift—mostly poets, who work with magic anyway. I think that Arnold Bennett came as close to defining it as anyone, when (in a letter to his friend, George Sturt) he said, "You are . . . a man that can see beautifully, and only wants practice to say beautifully what he sees beautifully." E.B. White has the ability to see beautifully, *and* over the years he has developed the ability to say beautifully. If you read his *Letters,* you will observe that these talents were there when he was young; they were *sui generis,* but time has polished them until they rise unconsciously to his lips. While, like any serious writer, he works over his manuscripts, his casual conversation is very much like his writing.

Today, those interested in written English demand the use of short, self-contained sentences. They usually point to Henry Thoreau as an exemplar. Certainly Thoreau could, and did, write in that fashion, but he was capable of much longer flights of thought and frequently indulged in them. E.B. White seldom does. His writing is deceptively simple and easy to read. One of his paragraphs may contain many sentences, but the reader is not conscious of it because the thoughts follow along smoothly, head to tail, like the geese in his pasture. Writing in this fashion is not easy, although it may seem so. It can easily develop into a staccato chatter, with sentences flying around the reader's ears like machine gun bullets. E.B. White's sentences do not. They float along like Louis in *The Trumpet of the Swan,* which is one reason his children's books are so popular. (Another is that fantasy comes naturally to him; most authors see only what is visible to the naked eye.)

Frequently I am asked what sort of man is E.B. White. This is not easy to answer, because the question is too general. Externally, he looks like other men. The picture of him on the dust jacket of *Essays* is a good likeness. His books, particularly *Letters,* tell a lot about him. He was born in Mount Vernon, New York, on July 11, 1899. (To some this may seem long ago indeed, but it does not impress me, because I was born almost exactly two years earlier.) From his letters you learn that he has been worrying about his health all his life, but in view of the number of birthdays he has accumulated, his ailments obviously have been something less than mortal. He smokes rarely, but he drinks gin, which those who also smoke rarely but drink gin might consider part of the reason for his longevity. They would be wrong, though, because his wife, Katharine, did smoke heavily and did not drink gin, and she lived to be eighty-three.

Boswell would not have said that E.B. White was a "clubable man." He is not a joiner and not very social. Although he does not socialize with the native population, neither does he, to any extent, with people "from away." The "summer" ladies hereabouts, as well as the "year-round summer people," seldom entice him from his home acres, much as they would like to. He is not burdened with any notion of class distinction. He is well known in the village and is generous in his financial help to local worthy causes. The villagers generally think of him as they would if they had the largest elm tree in New England within their borders. It has been said that he is known here as "Joel White's father" (Joel is E.B. and Katharine White's son and runs a boatyard here in town), but they know him also as a famous writer and are as proud to have him as they would be to have the elm tree. While they call him Mr. White to his face, they often refer to him as Andy behind his back. His full name(which he heartily dislikes) is Elwyn Brooks White, but he acquired the name Andy as a college freshman. Cornell's first president was Andrew D. White, and Andy was, as he says, "a nickname commonly bestowed on Cornell students named White, and it stuck." I never have heard anyone call him Elwyn, and I doubt he would respond to it.

E.B. White's native shyness—or, let us say, his reluctance to become involved with large groups of people—is not any indication of unfriendliness, but merely shows a preference for his own company. This I can understand because I have the same feeling. It must be true, however, that Katharine White's long illness kept him housebound more than otherwise would have been the case.

He has consistently refused to attend functions where he was being given an award—among them the Gold Medal for Essays and Criticism from the American Academy of Arts and Letters, the Laura Ingalls Wilder Award, the National Medal for Literature, the Presidential Medal of Freedom, and the Boston *Globe*'s Laurence Winship Award, among others. Even if he were to be given the Nobel Prize for Literature, which I think he deserves, I doubt he would attend the ceremony.

It is not possible to evaluate E.B. White's writing without at the same time considering Katharine White. No man can live with a woman for forty-eight years—least of all a woman of Katharine White's background, personality, and ability— and not be influenced by her. Speaking of his wife in an interview with the *Paris Review,* E.B. White said: "I have never seen an adequate account of Katharine's role with the *New Yorker.* . . . She was one of the first editors to be hired, and I can't imagine what would have happened to the magazine if she hadn't turned up."

It is commonly acknowledged that women mature more quickly than men, and if one also considers that Katharine White was five years older than her husband and that she was a woman of firm convictions and outstanding ability, one is left with the conclusion that had it not been for her, E.B.W.'s future might have been very different. I do not mean that she taught him how to write, but in their early days she certainly must have exercised her very considerable editorial talents in his behalf. In addition to her fine intellect, she was a woman of striking appearance, as early pictures of her indicate. I was privileged to know her only after she gave up most of her work with the *New Yorker* and was living in Maine, but she was as interested as ever in literary matters. She was always on the lookout for promising writers, and she helped and encouraged many, among them such diverse types as John Updike, S. J. Perelman, and Vladimir Nabokov. Here in our village she revitalized the local library, and I have several long letters written from Florida (she was a great letter writer) about the library work we were doing here.

It is said that if you scratch an Englishman, even one living in the heart of London, you will find a countryman. E.B. White was born near New York, and after his *wanderjahre,* which took him across the country in a Model T and to Alaska on a steamer, he lived for many years in Manhattan. I am sure he loved the city, because his affection shows through in "Here Is New York," but he, like the Englishman, was a countryman underneath. He has always kept a few animals around his place in Maine and is famous locally (and farther afield, through his writing) for his geese. A pig he once owned achieved, though its passing, an immortal niche in literature comparable to that of the unfortunate Chinese animal referred to in Charles Lamb's "A Dissertation Upon Roast Pig." E.B. White's essay, "The Death of a Pig," tells the story of his Maine pig. It fell ill, died, and was buried, so its owner never got to lick his fingers after burning them on the hot crackling—as did Lamb's little boy, who discovered that roast pork is superior to live pig. During the summer, passers-by usually can see a small flock of chickens in the field next to E.B. White's house—his first venture into husbandry. A couple of years ago, I helped renew his flocks after the depredations of some unknown marauder, probably a fox or coon. He also has had sheep and a steer or two (called "beef critters" around here) grazing in his pasture. When he gave up farming, except for chickens and geese, he told me he did so because it was no longer fun when you could not care for your animals yourself. I agree, for when I found it burdensome to be chasing my bull down the highway, I too found that the zeal had gone and gave up farming, except for sheep and hens.

I do not believe anyone would contest the statement that E.B.W. did his best work in Maine. Happiness in rural surroundings depends on an ability to appreciate the importance of small things. That ability shines through all his writing. The story "Coon Tree" is a good example—though "Coon Hunt" is better, but you will have to buy *One Man's Meat* to read it. I spoke to him once about that piece, and, with his facility for getting to the meat of things, he remarked that what impressed him most was the hunters' insistence on getting as far from home as possible.

The only problem with reading books by E.B. White is that one is spoiled for the work of less talented writers. My personal difficulty, though, is that his style is so gentle and persuasive that it is absorbed into my stream of thought by a sort of osmosis. I am fearful of using a thought of his, believing it to be my own.

If the fairies were to gift me with a single wish, it would be that I might come upon E.B.W. again all fresh and new, as I did forty years ago. Since that cannot be, I have placed *Essays* on my bedside table, where I shall read one a night as long as they last.

"S' Matter, Bub?"

Not long ago, my wife and I went very early in the morning into a Howard Johnson's restaurant for breakfast. The place was barely open, but a waitress came to our table with a smile and listened attentively as I explained that I wanted hotcakes—but not the BIG ones that are like featherbeds and suffocate me. She nodded gravely and presently returned with my wife's order of bacon and eggs, and then placed in front of me a very large plate in the middle of which were three minute hotcakes, each about the size of a dime, carefully piled upon each other. I looked at them. Helen looked at them. The waitress looked at us, and we all burst into laughter. Of course she had a regular order too, waiting on the serving tray, but my day was made.

If one were to judge mankind by the horror headlines in the newspapers or the pictures and reports on TV, one would conclude that the world was peopled by savages, but with the slightest encouragement, the ordinary everyday people you see will meet you more than halfway. One reads about a preponderance of murder, arson, rape, robbery, and deliberate violence, and, unhappily, much of it seems to occur in countries that boast most about their freedom. I am sure there is violence in the Communist countries of China and the USSR but not much is reported, and its absence is confirmed by returning travelers.

The inevitable conclusion is that the human race behaves best when it is disciplined. This is not an earthshaking discovery; intelligent people have realized for centuries that civilization is an easily ruptured veneer, and that once discipline is relaxed, the events that follow are predictable and inevitable. Violence feeds on violence, and if the less responsible members of society perceive it to be profitable and go unpunished, they are encouraged to continue in their ways. There is no mysterious reason for the lawlessness that prevails today. One does not need sociological studies or vast funding of investigative committees to find the cause. It is simply that for a generation we have neglected our duty to discipline our young *and* ourselves.

Hanging on the wall of my study is an old print published in Winchester, England, according to an Act of Parliament, 1740. It is entitled "A Piece of Antiquity." It depicts a strange figure of a man with a padlocked pig's snout, ass's ears, and stag's feet. He is armed with sword and buckler, and stands with one hand open and the other filled with tools. Beneath him is a Latin verse that begins, *Effigiem Servi si vis spectari PROBATI* (which translates to "A Trusty Servant's Portrait would you see") and goes on to describe his qualities, which include among other virtues neatness, the ability to keep confidences, submission to authority, courage, and willingness to work.

These verses were intended for the instruction of the scholars of Winchester College, where they appear on an interior wall. I do not know how long they have been there, but certainly for a very long time. The school was founded by William of Wykeham in 1387 at a location where another school had existed since even more ancient times. The point is that the boys attending this rather venerable institution of learning are taught early that being a faithful servant is a laudable accomplishment—a belief that seems to have gone out of style, leaving us with schools where the students instruct the masters and the masters encourage them to do so.

(William of Wykeham is remembered also for having said "Manners myketh man," a motto that pundits have been trying to read backward ever since.)

It would be a grave error to assume that because evil is so visible it is the permanent life style of more than an insignificant part of society. Most people are decent, honest, law-abiding members of the community, and amazingly considerate of their fellows. If at times they appear to be thoughtless and wanting in compassion, it is because their immediate responses are negative rather than positive, which is due to lack of training, not lack of sympathy.

Today, as in the past, the ordinary citizen is seldom involved in serious conflict with the law. Mr. Everyman's rare brushes with authority are usually connected with minor civil offenses, just as they always have been. We read in history of torture and other unusual punishments afflicted upon miscreants, but the ordinary citizen of ancient Greece or Rome or medieval Europe probably avoided conflict with authority about as successfully as we do.

What is not suffciently emphasized in our media today is that no matter where you go or what you do, you are, more often than not, met with courtesy, kindliness, and helpfulness.

I was driving along the Pennsylvania Turnpike in the vicinity of Harrisburg one evening. It was a filthy day. The road was covered with slush, and great sheets were thrown up by every passing vehicle. Presently the engine of my car began to sputter and then died, leaving me stranded on the shoulder. I had just time to exhibit appropriate signals of distress—handkerchief on radio aerial and hood up—when a huge tractor-trailer pulled in behind me. The driver, black and built in proportion to the size of his truck, climbed down and walked over.

"S' matter, bub?" he asked. I replied that I didn't know; there was plenty of gas and electricity, but the engine had just up and quit. He looked under the hood, took the patient's pulse, and announced his diagnosis: "Gas line plugged up." I thanked him and said I guessed I'd have to sit and wait for a state trooper to come by. "Oh no," said he. "Climb up and I'll take you to the barracks. It's about ten miles up the road. You may sit around here for a couple of hours and freeze your ass." He boosted me into the cab of the tractor and offered me a cup of coffee from an oversized thermos flask. He wanted to know where I lived, told me where he lived, and ten or fifteen minutes later deposited me in front of the State Police barracks and roared off into the night. I have a considerable affection for truck drivers.

I would not go so far as Will Rogers and aver that I never met a man I didn't like, but I would suggest that, on the whole, people are not worse than they appear, but better. Friendliness and compassion are there, and if we run a taut ship, so that the crew knows the orders of the day, those virtues will have a chance to take over. And for habitual offenders, there is always the brig.

Cursing As an Art

One day not long ago, I was out walking with my wife. We were headed for Naskeag Harbor, not that we wanted anything there but merely because any walk is improved by having an objective. As we passed a ramshackle sort of boatshed-cum-workshop along the way, we heard from within a howl of anguish, followed by a staccato repetition of a four-letter word that, even today, I prefer not to repeat in print. We did not stop to offer assistance but continued discreetly on our way, because it was obvious that the sufferer was in no mortal danger.

Profanity does not offend me when it is occasioned by a sterling demand for relief, as seemed to be the case here. After all, I consider myself to be fairly skilled in its use, having studied under masters of the art during my years at sea. No, I was not offended—but I was disappointed by my neighbor's limited vocabulary. As we moved far down the road, his voice, now but a faint echo, continued repeating that single word of one syllable that was all his limited talents could dredge up to express his woe.

Cursing is an art at which our forefathers, even unto my youth, were masters. True, the church has frowned upon the practice and driven some oaths (or what they considered to be oaths) underground, where they remain lightly camouflaged. In Maine, several have "passed" into the fold of respectability. One is the use of the word *baster* as descriptive of something large and stubborn to handle. A boulder that resists all normal attempts to move it could be an old baster, and baster is, obviously, a synonym for bastard. Another profanity in common use among the middle generation of Maine natives is *Godfrey Mighty,* which is equally clearly intended as a substitute for God Almighty.

In England the word *bloody,* which in this country merely indicates covered in blood, is a powerful oath not used in parlor company. Its origin reaches back to the eighteenth century, when young bucks swore by God's blood, abbreviating it and taming it a little by saying "'S blood." The English are still, I think, more artistic in their swearing than are we. One of their favorites I have always found entertaining is the insertion of bloody as an accent in a sentence, or even in a word. One frequently hears "not bloody likely," or "how bloody awful," but what particularly enchants me is "extrabloodyordinary." Like German, it is a language where you can make up your words as you go along.

The old English four-letter word for copulation is quite improper in polite society, but there are a number of euphemisms quite reasonably respectable. "Screwed up" is often used in the sense of things being confused, and is merely a substitute, changing the word but not the meaning. In their studied effort to be uninhibited, the young refer to copulation as "having sex," which is about as silly as one can imagine because everything has sex, male or female or neuter, and a number of languages do also—Spanish, for instance—in that their nouns have gender. Why the word for the sex act should have wound up as an obscene expression, when next to eating and sleeping it is the commonest and most pleasant of human occupations, I do not know. (Some might say it heads the list, but that is a question of age.)

Much of profanity is a matter of fashion. What is vulgar today may not have been yesterday, and will not be tomorrow. If you read Shakespeare or Pepys you will find that people in the sixteenth and seventeenth centuries commonly expressed themselves in words that we embarrassedly avoid today. The Bible itself provides many instances. Logically, it is all complete nonsense. Why should one say "have sex" instead of —————— ? Everyone knows what is meant, and there is nothing evil in words themselves.

Actually, skill in the use of profanity is only part of the phraseology of good, resounding curses. A really fine curse demands much more than the use of oaths; it needs a vivid imagination and the impromptu ability to put appropriate words together. Good curses come out of sudden need, and there is no time to compose them. They should burst from the heart, and flay and excoriate even as they amuse the bystander and relieve him who curses.

One of my favorite descriptions of a virtuoso at the art occurs in "The Jackdaw of Rheims," from the *Ingoldsby Legends,* which were written by a parson, the Reverend R. H. Barham, early in the last century. The situation described arose because a pet jackdaw had stolen the Cardinal's ring.

> . . . *The Cardinal rose with a dignified look,*
> *He call'd for his candle, his bell, and his book!*
> *In holy anger, and pious grief,*
> *He solemnly cursed that rascally thief!*
> *He cursed him at board, he cursed him in bed!*
> *From the sole of his foot to the crown of his head!*
> *He cursed him in sleeping, that every night*
> *He should dream of the devil, and wake in a fright;*
> *He cursed him in eating, he cursed him in drinking,*
> *He cursed him in coughing, in sneezing and winking;*
> *He cursed him in sitting, in standing, in lying;*
> *He cursed him in walking, in riding, in flying;*
> *He cursed him in living, he cursed him in dying! —*
> *Never was heard such a terrible curse!!!*
> *But what gave rise to no little surprise,*
> *Nobody seem'd one penny the worse!*

I am glad to say that the jackdaw did emerge repentant, but in sad shape from the curses, which had indeed had effect. He was, however, forgiven. The trouble with modern times is that nobody believes in the efficacy of curses, and as a consequence we are losing a colorful mode of expression. Part of our loss is due to people like Sir Walter Scott, who said somewhere in his voluminous writings: "Dinna curse him sir; I have heard it said that a curse was like a stone flung up to the heavens, and most likely to return on the head of him that sent it."

While curses do no material harm, they satisfy an inner need, and I am sure that if my neighbor had been possessed of more eloquence he would have been relieved sooner.

Disposable

Yesterday being bright and sunny, a good day overhead, as we say around here, Helen and I decided to go shopping. When you have to drive over one hundred miles round trip to your nearest big town to shop, you don't set off casually. We did not consult voodoo signs or wait for a propitious positioning of the stars, but we did listen to our "all-weather" radio and modify the official forecast with what experience has taught us about Maine weather. Being satisfied, we set off.

As always, there was a lot to be done. We needed a thermometer, a battery for the radio, an old-fashioned top-of-the-stove toaster, a couple of three-by-five file boxes, some Chinese cabbage, dried mushrooms (the kind called "wood-ears"), and various other exotics from the little Chinese food shop that is painted outside a startling lacquer red. We needed Black Leaf 40 to kill the bugs in the greenhouse, fresh haddock for supper, and the usual mountain of groceries from the supermarket—plus getting my hair cut (I still favor a 1930 Establishment trim that I can get only in the big town) and lunch. Eating lunch out, when you get to town only once in three weeks, is high adventure even if it consists only of a celebratory martini and a dish of ravioli.

The stovetop toaster needs a little elucidation. I'll tell you right off that such toasters are not easy to find in the 1980s, but if your search is successful, you will find that they cost a lot more than they did in times past. In my youth they cost twenty-five cents; however, the current model is improved and makes toast that tastes as good—or better—than does the fifty-dollar electric machine. Of course, the stovetop type won't broil cheese sandwiches or heat croissants, but on the occasions when one wants these they can be put under the broiler in the kitchen range for a few minutes.

Shortly after World War II, some friends talked me into joining them in investing in a company that was making electric toasters. We were going to make a fortune because our toasters popped down instead of up, obviously taking advantage of Newton's law of gravity rather than bucking it. What we hadn't taken into account was the perversity of human nature. People don't like to cooperate with nature and they don't think much of ideas that do. They want to prove that they are related to the rugged pioneers who conquered the purple West and went down fighting nature. Also, they don't admire having their toast slide out the bottom of the toaster onto the floor.

If I failed to make the promised fortune, I did learn something about electric toasters. I learned—though I cannot put my finger on any useful purpose this knowledge has served—that they are rather tricky machines. The heart of a toaster is the heating element, and the brain is a little gadget made of bi-metal that expands with heat and contracts with the lack of it. When such toasters work, they are fine, but they are subject to unexpected attacks of cussedness that it would take an electrical wizard from MIT to tame.

I had a friend who owned a pop-up toaster that either didn't pop at all, and in consequence turned the toast to a crisp, or else popped so successfully that it hurled the toast halfway across the room. When my friend's children were growing up, they would stand in depth, like baseball players fielding high flies, and take the toast on the wing. My friend, incidentally, is related to Edward Fitzgerald, he who translated the *Rubaiyat* of Omar Khayyam (which sings of a loaf of bread, a jug of wine, etc., but, sadly, says nothing about toast).

We have owned for several years two General Electric toaster ovens that, apart from the normal contrariness of things mechanical, have operated reasonably well. However, of late they have taken to toasting unevenly, or hardly at all, and giving forth small internal explosions of an alarming character. As an old toaster expert, I decided that a couple of new heating elements, and perhaps soldering of a loose connection, might insure them further years of life.

Accordingly, we loaded them into our VW and stopped first at an establishment that repairs vacuum cleaners and other electrical oddments. There, we were told by the pleasant gentleman who owns the place that much as he would like to help us, he couldn't. He would have to invest thirty thousand dollars in spare parts if he took on all brands of toasters, and he didn't have that sum to invest and doubted he ever would.

We stopped at another shop where we have been before and were told that GE had discontinued making parts for our models. All we could do, he said, was heave them out and buy new ones. I don't know if this is a deliberate attempt on the part of the manufacturer to promote new sales, or if they just do not want to be bothered with making repair parts, even though there must be thousands of these appliances still in use. I would guess that it is probably a little of both, but what I am sure of is that it reflects the incredibly wasteful philosophy that permeates our whole society today.

Not long ago, I asked a youngish man if he knew where I could find a cobbler. He looked at me, wanting to be helpful but puzzled by my question. I explained further and he answered, "Oh, you mean a shoemaker." I in turn replied, "No, I mean a cobbler, a man who *repairs* shoes. I don't want any shoes made." He told me there was none in town, and he was correct. I did run one down later in another town, but generally they are not to be found, whereas thirty or so years ago there was one in every half dozen blocks.

Well within my lifetime there was room in our society for a limitless number of people engaged in useful, individual, modest, daily pursuits. There was the rag, bottle, and bone man, who either pushed his cart or walked beside the ancient horse that drew his wagon. The man would weigh and buy on the spot almost anything anyone had decided to discard. Nobody called it recycling; such fancy concepts were left for the profligate future. There were the fish man, the baker, the milkman, the butcher, the tinker, and, in the country (where we still have a few), the store on wheels—all of whom came to our doors. The former owner of the farm where I live had his little store in front of the barn, but he too had a delivery wagon in which he called on shut-ins and various of his neighbors who for their own reasons did not want to go out to shop. There was also the knife and scissors sharpener, who, in the city, pushed his grinder along on its large wheel. It could be turned over so that, equipped with a belt and foot pedal, the large wheel drove a smaller one (attached to a grindstone) at a high rate of speed. In the country, a similar rig was often to be found in the back of a tinker's wagon. The tinker soldered and put patches on pots and pans that today we would throw away.

In Philadelphia, where my wife formerly lived, there were the pepperpot soup man, who sold you "Peppery pot, piping hot," and the peanut vendor with his whistle. One could also find the Hokey Pokey man, who sold water ices on which he would shake a colored syrup; the chestnut vendor, who did his best business on cold days, when people bought the hot chestnuts to keep their hands warm; and the soft pretzel man, who sold you a big pretzel slathered with mustard for a dime.

This was a society of small, frugal, happy people. A few got rich, but they were never anybody you knew, so it didn't matter. There were also the very poor, but most of us seemed to get along reasonably well within our place in the pecking order by not expecting too much. The affluent society had not yet been heard of, and if you had suggested it, people would have wondered what sort of racket you were trying to promote.

What marked the era was the opposite of affluence. It was economy, which was not, as most of today's citizens seem to believe, poverty. Only fools threw away things that were not worn out and could be repaired. We now live in strange times when our biggest problem is trying to dispose of the stuff people discard. We seem afflicted by some insanity, convinced that the way to happiness is through waste. The hallmark of excellence is the word *disposable*. If there is any way to make things cheaper (we seem to be saying) so that they will wear out faster and thus have to be thrown away and a newer model bought, let us do so. Looking around our house, I can see that those things a hundred or so years old will, with reasonable care, be around for another hundred, whereas most of what I have bought recently won't last out this century.

I doubt there was anything in my grandfather's house that could not be repaired, nor, though he was reasonably well-to-do, would he ever have thought of throwing away anything unless it was irretrievably broken. (Even then he would have kept the pieces around for a while to be sure some substitute use for them might not show up.) If I were able to tell my grandfather about my toaster ovens, I would refrain from doing so, for fear he would think I was losing my mind. He would not be able to understand why I would pay sixty dollars for something to toast bread by electricity when I could do the job equally well on the stove, and he just would not believe that I could not find anyone to repair a four-year-old toaster.

This is a phase of our national life that may pass. Few other peoples in the world are so wasteful. Even now, we can hear the rumbling of a distant drum as we awake to the fact that earth's riches are finite. The rumbling will continue, and we dare not—as old Omar suggested—"Take the Cash and let the Credit go, nor heed the rumble of a distant Drum." What we *can* do is mend our ways and learn from the experience of those who passed this way before us—to take pleasure from frugality rather than waste.

Your E String Is Flat

I have a new typewriter—a German Olympia, the only nonelectric type-writer available in the local office supply store. I learned to use a type-writer about sixty years ago, and have not advanced with the times. I think, but I'm not sure, that the first machine I ever used was an Oliver. As I recall through the haze of years, the arms carrying the type face arched over from the back when you pressed the keys. They reminded me of the bony fingers of Shakespeare's witches, dancing around the kettle over which they stretched their hands and chanted, "Double, dou-ble toil and trouble / Fire burn and cauldron bubble." In those days, the keys themselves often presented their own sort of trouble to my novice fingers. I suppose one would have to go to a museum to find such a machine today, although I remember it was highly thought of at the time. It probably was not the kind of writing equipment upon which one could knock out fifty words a minute, and it certainly didn't have a memory bank that could store and correct your copy—but since I was, and still am, a hunt-and-peck artist, it didn't make much difference.

I have not discarded my old Royal, because I realize it will be some time before Olympia will help me compose a worthwhile article. We are not yet acquainted and are like young lovers, enthusiastic but awkward. But that will pass, and by and by all will be comfortable and familiar. I suppose that non-writers do not know how much a cooperative type-writer means to an author. Lots of times it slips in a few words on its own to make a felicitous phrase that one didn't know about until after rereading the copy. At other times it makes obvious—so you can delete them—things that should not have been written in the first place. Of course, all typewriters have their foibles and idiosyncracies.

I often wonder about authors who wrote every word in longhand. I have seen some of their copy—Thoreau's, for instance. If the Interna-tional Typographical Union had been in business in his day, they would have called a strike rather than have to decipher his script. It was hieroglyphic, and after he had read it over and made numerous changes, as all writers do, it was illegible to anyone not inspired.

Nathaniel Hawthorne would have had trouble using a typewriter. I know because when I was shown the attic room of his house in Con-cord where he escaped to write, his desk was pointed out to me and I was told that he stood, rather than sat, at it to work. The desk was typi-cal early nineteenth-century bookkeeper's furniture, at which, I suppose, the scrivener (like those overworked drudges in Dickens's novels) usually sat on a high stool. When Hawthorne was tired of standing, he let himself out the back door and stretched his legs and mind by walking on top of the embankment behind the house.

I have always been hot and cold about Hawthorne. I like *Our Old Home,* and perhaps *The Scarlet Letter,* but the spooky ones I can leave by the wayside. He wrote *Our Old Home* while he was American consul in Liverpool, a job he was awarded as a quid pro quo by President Pierce in return for the book Hawthorne wrote about him. What I like best is the little scribble he wrote with his wife's diamond while they were honeymooning in the old manse in Concord. He obviously loved Sophia, and you can still see them standing by the window "in the gold light."

All I know about writing is that when I am trying hard to be literary nothing happens, but when my typewriter takes over and does the job for me, I am on the right track.

Most writers get asked about their work. People are curious as to how they do it—when and where they find the stuff they spin out of their heads as spiders spin webs. People seem curious about their personal lives too: what sort of lives they lead, and why they choose to write, and even how much they get paid (although most are too polite to ask). I have been the object of many such inquiries over the years, and can best answer by quoting a letter I received from a writer friend: "Writing is a disease and not a profession. But it has its rewards," he said, "provided one survives." He is right: if you contract the disease, it is incurable. You die, or you live with it.

Ever since I was a little boy, so entranced by whatever book I was reading that I was deaf to all commands, I have been writing. Not always on paper, but in my head, where all writing begins. I take a book to bed with me every night, and, after polishing my glasses and adjusting my bedside lamp, I begin to read. I never get far before something starts the wheels in my head turning and I am off on my magic carpet.

One of the reasons writers write is that they want to get at the center of things. As they go along, one word following another, little lights begin to flash, and if they follow them carefully, they are presently conscious of having discovered something they had not realized was there before. They are close to the center of whatever idea they have been seeking. A writer's function, as I see it (and a poet's too, to a greater degree), is to make visible something that has existed right along but has not yet been seen.

Of course, you can think that you've caught the nub of an idea, as I did one time when I handed my wife one of my minor masterpieces. She read with what I thought was deep appreciation, then finally looked up and said, without a tremor in her voice, "Your typewriter needs cleaning." It was as though Nero's wife, while he was fiddling over Rome's burning, had remarked, "Dear, your E string is flat."

Seven Years Boy

Nowadays, little boys grow old faster than they used to. Much more is done for them, and more thought is given to what is happening to them as they grow. Frequent television programs tell us about children's behavior and their mental and physical development at different ages. Parents can attend public education classes that alert them to what is happening to their progeny. Sex education—knowledge that one got by osmosis in the old days—is now taught in public schools. I suppose it is all right if that is what the parents who are paying the bills want, but I have not observed much improvement in the sexual mores of those exposed to it. The divorce rate is a good deal higher than it used to be, and as sex seems to be involved in most divorces, one could conclude that the principals have not lived happier sexual lives.

Children today are, I guess, healthier, although I cannot remember many of my playmates being *un*healthy. Of course we all got chicken-pox and measles and mumps, and the unlucky ones contracted scarlet fever and polio (only then it was called infantile paralysis). A few more must have died in those days, but as more young men have been senselessly slaughtered in wars in the last seventy-five years than died by disease in earlier years, I don't see how we are better off. War is an evil thing for many reasons, not the least being that it reverses the

Darwinian theory of the survival of the fittest. The fittest get killed, and the unhealthy specimens are left to breed. Maybe this helps explain why the extreme span of life has not been extended by modern medicine, just that more people live to be old.

Even with more senior citizens around, it seems that fewer little boys enjoy the companionship of older people. I was lucky, because I skipped a generation and was raised by my grandparents. For me, boyhood was a time of extraordinary wonder and delight. (I'm sure this applies to girlhood too, but I was never a little girl and so cannot vouch for it.) The days were endless—but never long enough. I was made to go to bed early, though I hated to, but allowed to get up at first light as long as I made no noise, which meant that in summer I was around early enough to see the family cow get milked and to learn how to do it. I was also allowed to shake down a little hay for the horses and scoop up a portion of oats for them in a wooden measure that was smooth with the use of years.

I walked to school of course; everyone did. It was about a mile to school, I guess. There were no buses, and even if there had been I doubt our elders would have consented to our riding on them. I doubt we would have wanted to either, after a few trial runs. There was so much to see and do as we walked. There were birds' nests to look for in the hedgerows, and crows' nests in the treetops that one could throw stones at, and the daub-and-wattle nests of swallows under the eaves of buildings. There were tadpoles in the ditches, and, in season, green apples to be stolen (the kind that Thoreau called *Cholera morbifera aut dysenterifera, puerulis dilectissima*). These could be thrown at something, or somebody, even if they were too sour to eat—which was hardly ever, boys' tastes being what they are.

Although I have lived to be old, the seven years of my boyhood seem, in retrospect, to have been longer than any other interval in my life. Seven years because, as the old saw has it, "Seven years baby, seven years boy, seven years hobbledehoy, and all the rest a man." No seven years since have encompassed such an eon. Perhaps, as Wordsworth said, it is because with increasing maturity "Shades of the prison-house begin to close / Upon the growing boy." I do not suggest that I was undisciplined, because discipline was more rigid in those days. I think, though, that less was expected of children in the way of early maturity. What was demanded was adherence to a code of manners that was never questioned, a code that did not have to be explained but rested merely upon accepted rules prohibiting certain things that simply "were not done." Within these limits we were as free as the birds whose nests we rifled.

I was reading an essay the other day in a book by Richard Jeffries entitled *Saint Guido*. It is a fantasy about a little boy named St. Guido. You will have to read the book yourself to find out why he was called Saint, but for now it is enough to say that St. Guido runs off to play in a wheat field. He has a number of small adventures, and by and by the wheat begins to talk to him:

> . . . if your people do not gather the flowers now, and watch the swallows, and listen to the blackbird whistling, as you are listening now while I talk, then, Guido, my love, they will never pick any flowers, nor hear any birds' songs. They think they will, they think that when they have toiled, and worked a long time, almost all their lives, then they will come to the flowers and the birds and be joyful in the sunshine. But no, it will not be so, for then they will be old themselves and their ears dull, and their eyes dim, so that the birds will sound a great distance off, and the flowers will not seem bright.

Spent Upon His Knees

We had the garden club ladies at our house yesterday, about fifty of them. They seemed, on average, to be on the shady side of forty. I didn't see many calluses displayed, though there were a few grubby fingers suggesting that their owners did handle "the good earth" in their spare moments. On the whole, though, I think that garden club ladies are more given to admiring flowers than to growing them. It is not my intention to be critical about either the ladies' ages or their lack of enthusiasm for weeding, squashing cutworms, or deadheading slimy day lilies. After all, Kipling said that "half a proper gardener's life is spent upon his knees," and I am afraid that if a lot of these champions of floriculture got upon their knees they might have difficulty getting up again. I know; though I have been gardening all my life, I go through some pretty fancy contortions regaining a vertical position after a few minutes with my nose to the ground.

The American attitude toward one's increasing years annoys me. If I ever mention age in my column someone is sure to say to me before the week is out, "You shouldn't say you are getting old!" Now, I really don't go around telling people I am growing old any more than I remind them that I have gray hair or an aquiline nose, because the evidence speaks for itself, but I don't avoid the subject either. The fact that every living thing grows older every day neither elates nor distresses me. There is nothing to be done about it, and from where I sit it has as many pluses as minuses. If I have learned anything by living as long as I have, it is that only fools waste their time and effort fighting the inevitable. Nobody has yet been able to avoid old age but by early death, so the obvious thing to do is ignore it and make all the hay you can while the sun shines. I have always liked what Bobbie Burns wanted as an epitaph on his tombstone—in fact, I have had it cut on mine. It goes:

If there's another world,
He lives in bliss,
But if there's not,
He made the best of this.

My small great grandson, Noah, said to me one day, "Is great-great grandmother getting ready to die?"

I replied, "No, not so far as I know; anyway, she has not said anything to me about it." When he said no more, I added, "Why? Has she told you she is?"

Noah answered, "No, but she *is* very old, isn't she?" To which comment I had to agree she was; that indeed in a little while she would celebrate her ninety-third birthday. He nodded his head in confirmation, then said, "I am five years old and I am going to camp on Tuesday." I assumed that so far as he was concerned the subject of great-great-grandmother's approaching demise had been disposed of satisfactorily.

Children view death differently from their elders. We allow ourselves to get distressed about it, but I am convinced from evidence that the event passes over children's heads lightly. They may be sad for the moment, but they have not spent a lifetime thinking about it. They take it as being as natural as the sunset. They hold the dead bird or the mouse rescued too late from the cat in their hands and decide to "make a funeral," and that is the end of it.

You will see that my cogitations about old age have finally gotten around to dying, because that is the outcome of old age that most people dislike. I guess what we all would like to avoid is the giving up of our accumulations, human as well as material. We dislike the thought of leaving those we love, though if we are given to even a modest degree of contemplation we have to admit that even the happiest of associations eventually fade in the memory of the living and are replaced by new ones.

On a material plane, I sometimes wonder what will happen to my library that I have spent fifty years accumulating. I dislike the thought of my books winding up on the dusty shelves of a secondhand bookstore, but I take comfort in the poem on Richard Le Galliene's bookplate, which reads in part:

> *Books I have loved so well, my love so true*
> *Tells me 't is time that I should part from you,*
> *No longer, selfish, hoard and use you not,*
> *Nor leave you in the unlettered dark to rot,*
> *But into alien keeping you resign —*
> *Hands that love books, fear not, no less than mine.*
> *Thus shall you live upon warm shelves again,*
> *and 'neath an evening lamp your pages glow,*
> *Others shall press 'twixt leaf and leaf soft flowers,*
> *As I was wont to press them long ago:*
> *And blessings be upon the eyes that rain*
> *A tear upon my flowers — I mean on "ours" —*
> *If happly here and there kind eyes shall find*
> *Some sad old flowers that I have left behind.*

What counts is what we leave behind, and worrying about being old isn't going to help a bit. If, by the time we are old, we have not been able to contribute some slim volume to the shelves of posterity, there is nothing to be done about it. Fortunately, almost all of us have, at some time, made our contribution, young or old. Let's heed old Omar, who wrote:

Ah, fill the cup:
— What boots it to repeat
How Time is slipping
  underneath our feet:
  Unborn To-morrow
  and dead Yesterday,
Why fret about them if To-day be sweet!